D1061873

The Murder of
Emmett Till

THE MURDER OF
EMMETT TILL

David Aretha

MORGAN
REYNOLDS
PUBLISHING

Greensboro, North Carolina

THE CIVIL RIGHTS MOVEMENT

The Trial of the Scottsboro Boys
Marching in Birmingham
Selma and the Voting Rights Act
The Murder of Emmett Till
Freedom Summer

THE MURDER OF EMMETT TILL

Library of Congress Cataloging-in-Publication Data

Aretha, David.
   The murder of Emmett Till / by David Aretha.
      p. cm.
   Includes bibliographical references and index.
   ISBN-13: 978-1-59935-057-8
   ISBN-10: 1-59935-057-2
   1. Till, Emmett, 1941-1955--Juvenile literature. 2. Till, Emmett, 1941-
1955--Influence--Juvenile literature. 3. Mississippi--Race relations--Juvenile
literature. 4. Lynching--Mississippi--History--20th century--Juvenile literature.
5. African Americans--Crimes against--Mississippi--History--20th century--
Juvenile literature. 6. African American teenage boys--Mississippi--Biography-
-Juvenile literature. 7. Racism--Mississippi--History--20th century--Juvenile
literature. 8. Trials (Murder)--Mississippi--Juvenile literature. 9. Civil rights
movements--Southern States--History--20th century--Juvenile literature. 10.
African Americans--Civil rights--Southern States--History--20th century--
Juvenile literature. I. Title.
   E185.93.M6A75 2007
   364.1'34--dc22

                                    2007026250

Printed in the United States of America
First Edition

Contents

Chapter One:
Summer Vacation 9

Chapter Two:
How It is Down South 16

Chapter Three:
The Abduction 36

Chapter Four:
North vs. South 51

Chapter Five:
The Trial 65

Chapter Six:
Repercussions Around the World 80

Chapter Seven:
The Killers Talk 92

Chapter Eight:
Rumblings 107

Chapter Nine:
The Movement 116

Chapter Ten:
Fifty Years Later 130

Timeline 138
Sources 140
Bibliography 150
Web sites 157
Index 158

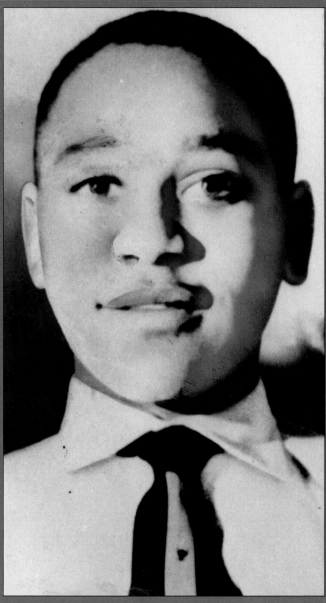

Emmett Till
(*Library of Congress*)

one
Summer Vacation

It was summertime in Chicago in 1955, and spirits ran high in Mamie Till-Bradley's household. A widow since World War II, Bradley mothered a gregarious, fourteen-year-old boy. His name was Emmett Louis Till, but his mom liked to call him Bobo—or simply Bo.

Employed by the Air Force since the war, Bradley did all right for herself. She had just bought a new car and, with a month of vacation time scheduled, planned to take a road trip to Omaha, Nebraska, with her son, mother, and boyfriend, Gene Mobley. Emmett, though, had different ideas. His great-uncle, Mose Wright—visiting Chicago to attend a funeral—charmed Emmett with tales about his beloved Mississippi: peaceful summer days, endless fields, and the best fishing one could hope for.

"Emmett got caught up in these images that Papa Mose created," his mother wrote. "For a free-spirited boy who

Emmett sits beside his mother, Mamie. *(Library of Congress)*

lived to be outdoors, there was so much possibility, so much adventure in the Mississippi his great-uncle described."

To Emmett, confined to the concrete and asphalt of Chicago's South Side, Mississippi indeed seemed like paradise. He also recalled his last visit to Mose and Elizabeth Wright's home at age nine, when he got to feed the cows and chickens that roamed their small parcel of land. When Emmett heard that his two cousins, Wheeler Parker and Curtis Jones, were going to visit Uncle Mose, it clinched the deal. Forget the road trip; Emmett was determined to go to Money, Mississippi.

For days, Bradley and her mother, Alma, opposed the trip, saying Emmett was too young to travel without them to Mississippi. But Emmett persisted, and, with Uncle Mose assuring her that Emmett and his cousins would be supervised at all times, she finally relented. Emmett, she said,

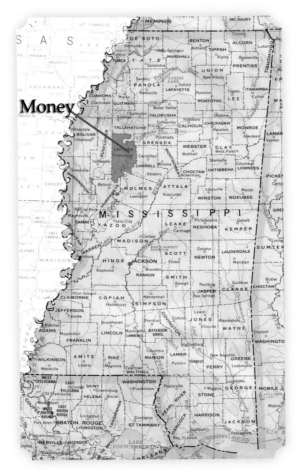

Emmett decided to go to his Uncle Mose's house in Money, a small town north of Greenwood, Mississippi. (*Courtesy of the University of Texas Libraries*)

could visit his relatives in Mississippi. Still, she warned him to mind his manners, especially around whites.

In Mississippi, Emmett met a white woman named Carolyn Bryant, and their meeting not only changed the lives of everyone around them, but it changed the course of America as well.

A petite woman who had won two local beauty contests, Carolyn Bryant, twenty-one, was married with two young sons. She operated Bryant's Grocery & Meat Market with her husband, Roy. A handsome man with thick, dark hair, Roy Bryant, twenty-four, had spent three years in the military as a paratrooper. Not well liked in his community, Bryant worked a second job as a truck driver to help pay his bills.

Because he was too poor to own a car, Bryant often borrowed the pickup of his half-brother, J. W. Milam. Nicknamed "Big," the balding thirty-six-year-old was a decorated combat veteran from World War II. Milam rented mechanical cotton pickers to plantation owners, and he prided himself on keeping local blacks in line through intimidation and cruelty.

J. W. Milam (left) and Roy Bryant *(Courtesy of AP Images)*

Milam intimidated such men as Mose Wright. Emmett's great-uncle, the sixty-four-year-old Wright shared a shack on a white man's plantation with his wife, Elizabeth, and his sons. Papa Mose, as he was called, preached in his local church, picked cotton, and made sure he and his family stayed out of trouble.

Mamie Carthan, Wright's niece, was born in the town of Webb, Mississippi, and moved with her parents, John and Alma, to a black neighborhood near Chicago at age two. Mamie committed herself to her studies and became the first black student at Argo Community High School.

In 1940, Mamie Carthan married Louis Till, who like her was just eighteen years old, and on July 25, 1941, they celebrated the birth of their child, Emmett Louis Till. A year later, however, the couple separated, and Louis Till died during World War II. In 1951, Mamie married Pink Bradley, but their marriage soon ended in divorce.

Despite such turmoil, Mamie provided the money and love that her son needed. She worked as a civilian procurement officer for the Air Force, earning a respectable $3,900 a year. After quitting time, she raced home to the boy she adored. "He was irresistible," she wrote about Emmett the toddler. "With his sandy hair and twinkling hazel brown eyes, he was the cutest little boy."

At age five, Emmett was stricken with polio. "He would go out and play every day, and at night he would burn up with fever," his mother said. The disease left Emmett with a permanent stutter, but otherwise he enjoyed a healthy childhood.

Talkative and full of energy, Emmett was a leader among his friends in their South Side neighborhood. "Emmett was a funny guy all the time," said Richard Heard, one of his classmates. "He had a suitcase of jokes that he liked to tell. He loved to make people laugh. . . . He made a lot of friends at McCosh Grammar School where we went to school."

Emmett loved baseball. When he wasn't rooting for his beloved Chicago White Sox and their star outfielder, Minnie Minoso, he would play ball with his buddies at Washington Park. His mother often drove a packed car of kids to the diamond, and sometimes she stayed to umpire their pickup games.

Emmett, in turn, helped his mother and neighbors with housework and chores. He cleaned his mom's apartment and washed their clothes. He painted a neighbor's hallway, helped others with their groceries, and shoveled snow during the cold Chicago winters. On many weekends, he visited his great-grandmother in Argo, where he helped her with cleaning and yard work.

By summer 1955, Emmett was a maturing adolescent, eager for independence. Though the trip to Omaha sounded fun initially, journeying to Mississippi with his cousin, Wheeler, seemed a lot more exciting. As the day of his train's departure approached, Emmett couldn't contain his excitement. He bought new clothes and shoes. He slipped on a ring left to him by his father, inscribed "LT: May 25, 1943." And he bought a new wallet, which came with a photo of Hedy Lamarr—a popular white actress of the day.

On Saturday, August 20, Mamie rushed to get Emmett to the Englewood train station, where the *City of New Orleans* was bound for Mississippi. By the time Emmett purchased his round-trip ticket, the engine's whistle blew and the conductor announced, "All aboard!" As he raced up the platform with his suitcase and box lunch (his mom's fried chicken), his mother grabbed his attention. "Bo," she said. "You didn't kiss me good-bye. How do I know I'll never see you again?"

"Aw, Mama," Emmett said. He gave her a departing kiss, then ran to catch up with Wheeler and Uncle Mose on the train. Emmett turned for a farewell wave and smile for his mother before disappearing from her view. Immediately, Mamie's spirits sank; she didn't know how she would last the week without her Bo.

two

How It is Down South

Bradley wanted her Bo to enjoy himself, but she had insisted he be careful around white people. In fact, she had drilled him on proper etiquette over and over again. Don't start a conversation with a white person, she told him. Only talk if you're spoken to. Say, "yes, ma'am" and "yes, sir." If a white woman is walking your way, she said, lower your head and step off the sidewalk. Don't even look at a *picture* of a white woman.

"If you have to humble yourself," his mother had said, "then just do it. Get on your knees if you have to."

"Oh, Mama, it can't be that bad," Bo replied.

"It's worse than that," she insisted.

Emmett assured his mother that he would heed her words. Yet Till was free-spirited and impulsive—and barely fourteen years old. Perhaps, his mother worried, he wasn't ready for Mississippi.

The Wright's home, outside Money, was located in the Mississippi Delta, an area about two hundred miles long and eighty miles wide in the northwest section of the state. The Delta—hot, muggy, and rural—epitomized the Deep South. Its flat, fertile land was ideal for agriculture, especially cotton, and for centuries plantation owners forced (and then employed for pitiful wages) large numbers of African Americans to work the land.

Map of the Delta region of Mississippi

As the train rolled through the Delta, Till saw signs announcing town names: Itta Bena, Yazoo City, Eden, and Tougaloo. He saw the many bare-wood shacks, home to African American sharecroppers and field hands who had been freed from slavery ninety years earlier. Till and his cousin eventually made their way to the Wrights' home near Money, which a welcoming sign boasted was "A Good Place to Raise a Boy."

Money, a Leflore County town that was home to just a few dozen people, was nestled between Old Money Road and the railroad tracks. The town's main feature was its cotton gin, a large building that stored equipment that helped process harvested cotton. One gas station and three stores lined Old Money Road, including Bryant's Grocery & Meat Market. A small elementary school stood behind the railroad tracks, and a smattering of houses could be found nearby.

As he traveled to his uncle's home, Emmett saw the sharecroppers' cabins that dotted the cotton fields of rural Mississippi. (*Library of Congress*)

Mose's home, where Emmett stayed during his trip to Mississippi *(Courtesy of the* Chicago Defender*)*

Mostly, though, the area was dominated by cotton fields, which seemed to go on forever. Shacks of various sizes dotted the fields. Mose Wright and his wife, Elizabeth, lived on a white man's 150-acre cotton plantation. They had one of the biggest homes of all the black field workers, boasting four bedrooms. Maurice, Robert, and Simeon—Emmett's cousins—lived in the house, too. During his stay, Emmett shared a bed with twelve-year-old Simeon, Mose's son. Wheeler, who was visiting with Emmett from Chicago, crashed at the Wright's, too. Another cousin from Chicago, Curtis Jones, was scheduled to visit in a few days.

For a black man in the Delta, Mose was fairly successful. He owned a half-acre of land near the edge of the cotton fields. In their garden, Mose and Elizabeth grew more than ten vegetables, such as lettuce, tomatoes, butter beans, and sweet potatoes. Mose's cow provided milk for the family, while the hogs would be slaughtered for meat later in the year. Many of his chickens laid eggs, while some were eaten

Mose Wright, Emmett's uncle *(Library of Congress)*

for special meals. Back in Chicago, Bradley envisioned Bo running around with his cousins trying to grab a chicken for Sunday dinner.

Despite the often oppressive heat, the sounds of the area were enchanting. Mockingbirds sang, locusts hummed, and soft breezes fluttered the leaves of the pecan, persimmon, and cottonwood trees. Nighttimes outside Mose's house were nearly pitch-black, lit only by the stars above.

On Monday morning, however, Emmett experienced the harsh reality of plantation life. All the young men had to help pick cotton, including the Chicago boys. While others had been known to pick up to four hundred pounds of cotton in a day, Emmett on Monday quit after twenty-five pounds. For the rest of the week, he helped Aunt Elizabeth around the home—washing clothes, cleaning the house, and tending to the vegetable garden.

Since it was the beginning of the picking season, workdays were shorter, and Emmett's cousins called it quits in the late afternoons. After work, they swam in the lake near their house and sometimes ventured down to the Tallahatchie River to fish. Lacking fishing poles, they slipped bait into jars and hoped the bass and catfish would wiggle their way inside.

Often at night, the family gathered around the radio to listen to shows like *Gunsmoke* and *The Lone Ranger*. Emmett dazzled his cousins with his own tales of Chicago. "Oh, that boy was a talker," said Bradley. "There was Riverview Amusement Park with all the great rides and the roller coaster. Oh, Chicago had the biggest this and the best that, to hear Emmett tell it, and he told it in a way that made everyone believe it. His cousins were awestruck."

Emmett loved the attention, not only from his cousins but from other young people in the area as well. To the town's children, the sharp-dressed Northerner with the fantastic tales was a novel attraction. Over the first several days of his visit, Emmett became confident, even brazen. But on Wednesday evening, he went too far—at least, that is, for a black youth in Mississippi. What Emmett did that night led to his death. Had he known the full history and extent of race relations in the South, he likely wouldn't have been so bold.

In the United States in the 1950s, two types of segregation existed: *de facto* (by custom) in the North and *de jure* (by law) in the South. All of the major northern cities, including Till's Chicago, experienced *de facto* segregation. Whites, believing African Americans would ruin, devalue, and/or overcrowd their neighborhoods, schemed to keep blacks away. As a sign in Detroit stated in the 1940s, "WE WANT WHITE TENANTS IN OUR WHITE COMMUNITY."

Most public facilities in the South were segregated at the time Emmett visited his uncle. *(Library of Congress)*

In many white neighborhoods, real estate agents refused to show homes to black buyers. When William and Daisy Myers, an upstanding African American couple, moved into Levittown, Pennsylvania, in 1957, whites stoned their house and burned crosses on their lawn. One resident wrote the governor, "If you had ever lived near those savages, then you would know why people would object to their moving into Levittown."

Because of such widespread racism, most northern blacks were confined to all-black communities. Hence, African Americans learned in all-black schools, which were frequently underfunded by whites in the state legislature. In many instances, northern white employers refused to hire black workers. Moreover, money lenders considered African Americans a bad risk, making it difficult for them to get a mortgage or a small-business loan.

Though northern *de facto* segregation was blatantly unfair, it paled compared to conditions in the southern states. The South's system of segregation, known popularly as Jim Crow laws, dated back to the 1800s. (Originally, Jim Crow was a bumbling black caricature made popular in minstrel shows.)

On January 1, 1863, during the middle of the Civil War, President Abraham Lincoln issued the Emancipation Proclamation. He declared "that all persons held as slaves" within the rebellious southern states "henceforward shall be free." On January 31, 1865, Congress passed the Thirteenth Amendment to the Constitution, officially abolishing slavery.

Federal government officials at the time were not naive. They knew that southern whites—who deemed blacks as inferior and who relied on their free labor to support their livelihoods—would resist the new amendment. Thus, during the era of Reconstruction, federal government officials and troops permeated the South. They oversaw the construction of black schools and ensured that African Americans were granted the right to vote. Many southern blacks even replaced many former Confederates in public office.

In 1868, Congress passed the Fourteenth Amendment, granting full citizenship to all people born or naturalized in the United States. The Fifteenth Amendment, passed in 1870, guaranteed voting rights to all adult male citizens. African Americans were further encouraged by the passing of the Civil Rights Act of 1875, which prohibited discrimination in public facilities.

Yet for northern white legislators, black freedom was merely a principle they believed in. For southern whites, it was a direct threat to the southern way of life, rooted in tradition for generations. Many considered blacks as inferior, and black males as sexual predators sexual predators. So while northern congressmen eventually tired of black issues—federal troops left the South in 1877—many Southerners remained committed to oppressing black citizens.

As early as 1865, legislatures in former Confederate states enacted "black codes." African Americans could not rent land, serve on juries, bear arms, assemble except for religious purposes, drink alcohol, travel, or learn to read. In 1866, the Ku Klux Klan was formed in Pulaski, Tennessee. Members harassed and attacked African Americans and those involved in Reconstruction.

All the while, the U.S. Supreme Court rendered several decisions that undermined Congress's civil rights laws. In

This Klansman displays a noose in an attempt to discourage blacks from voting. *(Library of Congress)*

1876, for example, it ruled that citizens could be denied the right to vote if they didn't meet certain criteria. And in 1883, the high court decided that while *states* were constitutionally bound to respect the rights of black Americans, *individuals* were not under such obligation. Thus, southern whites had the will and the means to continue to oppress African Americans.

Sharecropping was a particularly effective method of oppression. Plantation owners rented their land to free blacks, who harvested and sold their crops. However, black workers had to pay so much to the plantation owners—for rent, farming equipment, and food—that they were perpetually in debt. Moreover, many black men were arrested for small infractions, such as loitering, then forced to serve as free laborers for a white landowner. To African Americans, such a system was not much better than slavery.

Beginning in 1870, southern state legislatures began to pass Jim Crow (segregation) laws. These laws mandated that public facilities be separate for blacks and whites. A Tennessee law, for example, required railroad companies to furnish separate cars for black passengers. Inevitably, the white facilities were better funded and far superior to the black facilities.

Throughout the South, seemingly everything became segregated: schools, parks, streetcars, restaurants, outhouses, drinking fountains, swimming pools, and so on. The intensity of southern racism was evidenced by the minutiae of the laws. In South Carolina, African Americans were forbidden to play checkers with whites or look out the same factory window together. In Louisiana, the black ticket window at a circus had to be at least twenty-five feet apart from the white one.

Besides following such laws, black Southerners had to adhere to certain customs—ones that Bradley had warned Emmett about. While whites called a black man "boy," blacks had to address a white man as "Mister." Blacks had to step off the sidewalk if a white person was coming their way. In stores, a black person had to place money on the counter to

Under Jim Crow law, blacks were not allowed to drink from the same water fountains as whites. *(Library of Congress)*

avoid touching the salesperson's hand. Such customs were humiliating, oppressing African Americans emotionally as well as legally.

Instead of overturning segregation laws, the U.S. Supreme actually gave them its stamp of approval. In *Plessy v. Ferguson* (1896), the court stated that the segregation of public facilities was indeed constitutional as long as the facilities were equal. In the decades that followed, the South claimed it had "separate but equal" facilities when it was painfully obvious that the black facilities were almost always inferior. While white students were educated in decent schoolhouses, many black students learned in crowded, one-room, drafty shacks.

Wrote Pauli Murray in *Proud Shoes: The Story of an American Family:*

> Our seedy run-down school told us that if we had any place
> at all in the scheme of things it was a separate place, marked

off, proscribed and unwanted by the white people. We were bottled up and labeled and set aside—sent to the Jim Crow car, the back of the bus, the side door of the theater, the side window of a restaurant. We came to understand that whatever we had was always inferior.

Moreover, southern blacks had no chance of changing things through the power of the vote. Southern states devised clever schemes to circumvent the Fifteenth Amendment. In some states, citizens were required to pay poll taxes or pass tests in order to vote, and the questions were outrageously difficult.

Even if a black man paid his poll tax and passed such a test, he risked his livelihood and life if he tried to cast his ballot. Many African Americans who voted were fired or blacklisted by the whites in their community. Many others were threatened, beaten, or even killed for voting. Whites could murder African Americans knowing they would get away with it. Even if their case went to trial, all-white juries certainly would acquit them.

In Elaine, Arkansas, in 1919, black sharecroppers tried to unionize, but the white community would have nothing of it. After a church meeting of unionized sharecroppers was stormed by a group of white officials, a riot ensued. Several hundred armed whites roamed the countryside, hunting African Americans. Approximately two hundred people were killed.

Many times, whites abducted and lynched an African American for an infraction large or small. One black person was killed for frightening children by shooting at rabbits. According to the Tuskegee Institute, 3,386 black people were lynched from 1882 through 1930. Lynching took on many forms, including hanging, shooting, beating, and even roasting over slow fires. Sometimes, a lynching was scheduled and treated as a festive occasion. White people came to take pictures, picnic, and grab parts of the victim's body as souvenirs.

While segregation, lynchings, and the other injustices continued in the South for decades, relatively few Northerners voiced objections. In 1922, a bill would have made lynching a federal offense, but it never passed. In the 1915 film *The Birth of a Nation,* a virginal white woman commits suicide to prevent herself from being raped by a black male predator. The Ku Klux Klan, glamorized in the film, comes to the rescue. President Woodrow Wilson allegedly said the film was like "history written with lightning" and that it was "all so terribly true."

In the early 1900s, some African Americans, mostly in the North, began to take action. The National Association for the Advancement of Colored People (NAACP), formed in 1909, fought for black causes. In northern cities in the 1930s, protesters staged a "Don't Buy Where You Can't Work" campaign, pushing white employers to hire black workers.

After fighting for their country in World War II, African Americans found white Northerners more sympathetic to their cause than they had been before the war. In 1947, Jackie Robinson was accepted as the first black player in Major League Baseball. In 1948, President Harry Truman outlawed segregation in the U.S. military. In the South, however, Jim Crow continued to rule—especially in the Mississippi Delta.

Not only did Mississippi's textbooks glorify the Old South, but they were stored in segregated warehouses. Mississippi State University didn't just ban African Americans from its sports teams, it declined invitations to play in the NCAA basketball tournament because teams in the tourney had black players. Moreover, while only 20 percent of southern blacks were registered to vote in the 1952 elections, only 4 percent of black Mississippians were registered.

Mississippi had the lowest per-capita income in America, and Talahatchie County—where Till was visiting—was the sixth-poorest county in the state. The average white person in Talahatchie County went to school for less than six years, and African Americans averaged less than four years of education. While lynchings had all but disappeared in Mississippi by the 1950s, whites still ruled with the whip. Just weeks before Till arrived in Money, a girl was flogged for standing too close to a white woman in a store.

On Wednesday evening, Emmett was largely unaware of such history as he attended the local black church where Uncle Mose was preaching. Midway through the sermon, Emmett, his cousins, and other teens snuck out of the church and drove to Old Money Road, where they pulled up to Bryant's Grocery & Meat Market. Curtis Jones, Emmett's cousin from Chicago who recently came to stay with the Wrights, was among the group.

The store catered to the local black field hands. They bought penny candy and soda pop, and they hung out on the porch most every evening, playing checkers, listening to music, or just talking. About a dozen people, mostly young males, were gathered outside the store when the Wright truck arrived at about 7:30.

Emmett began telling stories about Chicago, and this time he had visuals. Till pulled a photograph out of his wallet. It was the photo of actress Hedy Lamarr, sold with his new

Bryant's Grocery & Meat Market *(Courtesy of the Chicago Defender)*

wallet, but Till claimed she was a white girl he personally knew. That got the crowd buzzing. One of the local boys pointed to the market. "Hey, there's a [white] girl in that store there," Jones recalls the boy saying. "I bet you won't go in there and talk to her." Another asked Emmett if he was chicken.

Full of confidence, and unaware of the consequences others blacks had faced just for associating with whites, Emmett accepted the dare. Everyone watched in anticipation as he pushed through the door.

Though the kids peered inside the windows, only two people knew what was said inside the store: Till, whose account would never be documented, and Carolyn Bryant. Carolyn was working the store alone that evening because her husband, Roy, was out of town, carting shrimp to Texas. Juanita Milam, the wife of Roy's half-brother, J. W. Milam, was in an apartment in the back of the store, oblivious to what was going on.

According to Carolyn Bryant's later testimony, Till asked for some bubble gum, which she got for him. But when she held out

Carolyn Bryant *(Courtesy of AP Images)*

her hand for money, Emmett grabbed it. As she pulled away, he said—according to Bryant—"How about a date, baby?"

Startled by the proposition, especially from a black male, Bryant turned and started toward the back of the store, toward the apartment. Till then stopped her near the cash register and put his hands on her waist. According to Bryant, Emmett asked, "What's the matter, baby, can't you take it?" Bryant pushed out of his grasp. At that point, she claimed Till said "unprintable" words to her. She said the last thing he told her was, "I been with white women before."

Peering inside, the youths realized that the Chicago kid had gone too far. One of his cousins ran in and pulled him

MISSISSIPPI COMMANDMENT

This advertisement for the NAACP depicts an African American boy being threatened by a white man for whistling. *(Library of Congress)*

out of the store. At the same time, Carolyn Bryant ran out of the market and toward the Milams' truck, where she grabbed a pistol. As the youths led Till to their own pickup, Bryant said that Till said "bye, baby."

Bryant also said that Till whistled at her. Whether or not he whistled is uncertain. Jones later said that Till did not whistle; other witnesses said he did. Emmett's mother would claim later that the crowd mistook his stuttering for a whistle. Years later, she offered a different explanation: When the kids asked him how he liked the woman in the store, he whistled his approval—to the guys, not at Bryant.

Whether or not he whistled, Till had seriously breached Mississippi's racial caste system. As they motored back to the church, the kids were abuzz about what had happened, and what *might* happen. What if Carolyn Bryant called the police? What if she told her husband? And what would Uncle Mose do if he found out? He was known to whip his young cotton pickers if they didn't work hard enough. What would he do to Emmett for this flagrant offense? And what would Emmett's mother do when Mose told her? According to a girl in the car, Emmett begged them not to tell Uncle Mose.

Meanwhile, Carolyn Bryant discussed the incident with Juanita Milam. Though Carolyn was obviously upset, they agreed not to tell their husbands about it, fearing they would overreact. So, when J. W. Milam stopped by an hour later, the two women remained hush.

Despite Carolyn's and Till's wishes, word of the incident spread like wildfire the next day, Thursday. Nothing like this had ever happened in Money, and gossip spread fast in the tiny town. Uncle Mose and Aunt Elizabeth heard the news on Thursday, too. They were scared for Emmett and talked about sending him on the next train home. However, when the sun set on Thursday evening and no whites had sought retribution, Mose and Elizabeth believed that the incident might just blow over.

Roy Bryant, though, didn't get back to town until 4 a.m. on Friday. He immediately went to bed, but by midday he headed for work at Bryant's Grocery & Meat. That afternoon, Emmett's sixteen-year-old cousin, Maurice Wright, betrayed his relative from Chicago. Maurice, who journalist Crosby Smith said resented Emmett's fancy Chicago ways, told Bryant all about the incident between Till and his wife.

"You see, here was this Chicago boy, dressed in fine clothes and carrying a little money in his pocket," Smith said. "I don't think Maurice liked Emmett much, but I don't guess he figured what was going to happen to him, either."

Roy Bryant confronted Carolyn about the story. She admitted it was true but pleaded that he just let it drop. But Bryant, as a proud, southern white man, felt obligated to take action. To defend white womanhood, to maintain white supremacy, to show local blacks the consequences they faced for defying codes of conduct, Bryant vowed revenge. His mind was made up.

three

The Abduction

Even before Emmett Till unknowingly transgressed racial codes, it was a particularly bad year for race relations in Mississippi. In 1955, Southerners were extra sensitive to challenges to their racial caste system, and especially angry with northern agitators—their word for civil rights advocates. The reason lay in a U.S. Supreme Court decision delivered on May 17, 1954.

In *Brown v. Board of Education of Topeka,* the Supreme Court overturned the "separate but equal" ruling of *Plessy v. Ferguson* (1896), which had legitimized segregation. In the *Brown* decision, the high court, led by Chief Justice Earl Warren, ruled that segregation in public schools was unconstitutional. Legal historians have called the ruling the most important Supreme Court decision of the 20th century, and it was an extraordinary victory for attorney Thurgood Marshall, lead counsel on the case, and African Americans everywhere.

George E. C. Hayes, Thurgood Marshall, and James Nabrit shake hands after the Supreme Court ruled in *Brown v. Board of Education* that "separate but equal" public schools were unconstitutional.

Many white Southerners, however, were outraged, referring to the day of the decision as "Black Monday." They believed that the U.S. government and northern agitators were out to destroy the southern way of life. Many were repulsed by the thought of integrated schools. As President Dwight Eisenhower himself said in a private conversation with Judge Warren, Southerners were "concerned lest their sweet little girls be seated alongside some big black bucks."

Eisenhower indeed captured the sentiments of the South. The *Jackson Daily News,* a newspaper in Jackson, Mississippi, said:

> Human blood may stain Southern soil in many places because of this decision but the dark red stains of that blood will be on the marble steps of the United States Supreme Court building. White and Negro children in the same schools will lead to miscegenation. Miscegenation leads to mixed marriages and mixed marriages lead to mongrelization of the human race.

Beyond the fear of integrated schools and mixed marriages, Southerners worried about the end of segregation in general. African Americans would swim in their pools, share public restrooms, and work beside them in stores and offices. Eventually, plantation owners would lose their cheap labor. And if all black citizens were allowed to vote, they would elect black councilmen, mayors, senators, and maybe even governors.

Southern leaders would not sit back and let that happen. In a meeting in Richmond, Virginia, on June 10, 1954, southern governors vowed to defy the *Brown v. Board of Education* decision. On July 7, 1954, the Louisiana state legislature voted to maintain its segregated public school system. On January 23, 1955, the Georgia Senate in a unanimous vote approved a bill that barred state funds to integrated schools.

White citizens did their part to support the cause. In July 1954, in Indianola, Mississippi, Robert Patterson formed the White Citizens' Council. The WCC was determined to use economic pressure to maintain segregation and keep African Americans off the voting rolls. If a black man was registered to vote, or if he was active in civil rights causes, the council would financially ruin him. If he owned a small business, for example, local whites would terminate his lease or persuade wholesalers to stop providing him goods. In the mid-1950s, White Citizens' Councils spang up throughout the South.

Because of such backlash, conditions for southern blacks actually worsened in the aftermath of the *Brown* decision. Prior to the ruling, 265 African Americans were registered to vote in the three Delta counties. By summer 1955, the figure had dropped to ninety. While 22,000 African Americans were registered to vote in Mississippi in the 1952 elections, only 8,000 were registered in 1956. Some counties had no blacks registered at all.

Even southern judges were determined to maintain white supremacy. In response to *Brown*, Mississippi Judge Tom P. Brady wrote in his booklet *Black Monday* that race mixing would ruin the nation. He also made a prediction:

> The fulminate which will discharge the blast will be the young negro schoolboy, or veteran who has no conception of the difference between a mark and a fathom. The supercilious, glib young negro, who has sojourned in Chicago or New York, and who considers the council of his elders archaic, will perform an obscene act, or make an obscene remark, or a vile overture or assault upon some white girl.

Brady's widely read booklet strongly influenced southern whites. Even those who didn't read it were wary of any black person with a northern accent. After all, the northern African American could be an activist with the NAACP (which some southern whites called a communist organization). He or she might be an investigative reporter for a northern black newspaper, such as the *Chicago Defender* or

Mississippi Judge Tom P. Brady wrote *Black Monday,* a widely read booklet that denounced desegregation. *(Library of Congress)*

Pittsburgh Courier, which railed for black rights. He or she might start filling the heads of southern blacks with notions of freedom and revolution. Whatever his or her intentions, a northern black surely meant trouble.

When Bradley sent her son, Emmett, to Mississippi, she

didn't realize the intensity of hostilities in the Magnolia State. In 1955, whites murdered two black activists, Lamar Smith and Reverend George Lee, each of whom had urged local blacks to vote. Smith was shot in broad daylight on the lawn of the Lincoln County courthouse. Though many bystanders saw the murder, the perpetrators were set free because no witness would testify.

It was within this hostile atmosphere that Emmett Till allegedly made his flirtatious gesture. But it seemed that Emmett had gotten away with it; there was no sign of retaliation on Thursday or Friday, and Emmett Till and his family were ready to put the incident behind them.

On Saturday evening, Bryant, after working all day at his grocery store, asked his half-brother, J. W. Milam, if he could borrow his truck. He told Milam what had happened between Till and his wife. Milam was so incensed that he insisted on joining Bryant on his visit. Milam, a war veteran, prided himself on his ability to keep blacks in line. He and Bryant agreed to visit Till together at Mose Wright's shack.

Meanwhile, Emmett had been taken to visit Greenwood, a town twelve miles away, by his cousins Maurice and Wheeler. While driving home that night on a dark road, Maurice accidentally struck an animal—most likely a dog. Emmett was shaken, and he pleaded with Maurice to stop the car. But the older cousin knew better. If the authorities discovered that they had killed a dog on a late-night drive—even by accident, and even if they turned themselves in—they could be severely punished by white authorities.

Maurice kept driving. Emmett, his pleas unheeded, began to cry. He cried for much of the trip home while the other boys sat in uncomfortable silence. Soon after they arrived home, Emmett and his cousins went to bed, hoping to sleep off the unpleasant experience.

At about 2 a.m., Milam and Bryant pulled up in their pickup truck to Mose Wright's property. Milam had turned off his headlights so as to avoid attention. One other person was in the truck with them, and another, a black man, was sitting in the back.

Milam, with a pistol in one hand and a long flashlight in the other, walked with Bryant to the house. Bryant pounded on the door.

"Who's that?" said Mose Wright from inside.

"Mr. Bryant, from Money, Preacher," said Bryant.

"All, right, sir. Just a minute." Wright opened the door.

"Preacher, you got a boy from Chicago here?" asked Bryant.

"Yes, sir," Wright said.

"I want to talk to him."

"Yes, sir. I'll get him."

Wright led Milam and Bryant to the back bedroom, where Emmett and three others were roused from their sleep. Milam shined his flashlight in Emmett's face.

"You the nigger who did the talking?" Milam demanded.

"Yeah," Till said.

"Don't say 'yeah' to me: I'll blow your head off. Get your clothes on." Till pulled on his pants and shirt, then reached for his socks.

"Just the shoes," Milam ordered.

"I don't wear shoes without socks," Till said.

Once he was dressed, Milam and Bryant pushed him toward the front door. Mose and his wife, Elizabeth, begged for mercy.

"He ain't got good sense," Mose said. "He didn't know what he was doing. Don't take him."

"I'll pay you gentlemen for the damages," Elizabeth said.

With the monetary offer, "Roy Bryant kind of hesitated," recalled Simeon. "But J. W. Milam, he didn't hesitate at all. He didn't even think about taking money. He came there to take Emmett, and that's what he proceeded to do."

Milam and Bryant led Till toward the door. On their way out, Milam turned and asked Mose how old he was. When he responded sixty-four, Milam replied that if he told anyone what had just happened, he wouldn't live to be sixty-five.

Milam and Bryant asked the person in the truck (most likely Carolyn Bryant) if Till was the right one. When the person said yes, they shoved Emmett into the back of the pickup. The black man, called "Wiggins" (by author Olive Arnold Adams, in her recreation of the event) was ordered to stay in the back with Emmett and hold him down.

After Milam drove away, the truck was spotted later that night in Money. Then it was seen in nearby Glendora. The woman was no longer in the truck, but four white men were—and all seemed to be inebriated. "Wiggins" was struggling to keep Till from getting away, so the men stopped at an African American nightspot to pick up another black youth, whom Adams called "Herbert."

At about 6 a.m., the pickup motored into Sunflower County, about twenty-five miles from Glendora, and arrived at a plantation owned by Milam's brother, Leslie Milam. At

Milam and Bryant beat Emmett inside this barn on Leslie Milam's plantation. *(Courtesy of Ed Clark/Time Life Pictures/Getty Images)*

the same time, an eighteen-year-old field hand named Willie Reed was walking across the plantation on the way to the country store. As the truck rolled toward the plantation's main barn, Reed got a good look at two of the four white men and stared right at the face of Emmett Till, who sat in the back between "Wiggins" and "Herbert."

The men entered the barn while Reed continued to cross the field. Soon he heard a young voice crying from inside the barn: "Lord, have mercy! Mama, save me!" Reed also heard heavy blows to a body. He heard cursing and yelling: "Get down, you black bastard!"

Frightened, Reed detoured to the home of Amanda Bradley, his aunt, about a hundred yards from the barn. He asked her who they were beating in there. Bradley knew that the Milam brothers were famous for pistol-whipping blacks. Willie's news of a beating didn't surprise her, and she tried to downplay it. Willie replied that it sounded like they were beating somebody to death.

Amanda Bradley asked Reed to fetch her some water from the well. He was too scared to go, but a family friend accompanied Willie to the well. On the way, they heard more cries, more blows to the body. While they drew water at the well, the cries grew fainter and then died out.

Willie Reed and his companion retreated to the house, where they and Mrs. Bradley watched the rest of drama from their kitchen window. J. W. Milam went to the well to get a drink, then walked back to the barn. The other three white men joined him in discussion outside the barn. One of them then drove the truck up to the barn's side door. The men carried what appeared to be a body through the barn's door and placed it in the back of the truck, then covered it with a tarpaulin. As the men got in the truck and drove away, the witnesses in the kitchen detected movement under the tarpaulin. That is the last they saw of the men that day.

Later, another black boy saw the truck. He noticed blood stains in the back and inquired about them. "I just killed a deer," was the response. The boy also noticed a pile of clothes near the barn. He was sent on an errand, and when he returned the garments were reduced to ashes.

Back at the Wright's home on Sunday morning, Mose and his family fretted and prayed for Emmett's return. Fearing for their safety, Mose didn't call the police. But Curtis Jones, Emmett's cousin from Chicago, couldn't wait any longer. He went to a neighbor's home and phoned his mother, Willie

Mae Jones, in Chicago. Someone also notified the sheriff. When Willie Mae Jones heard the news, she prepared to call Emmett's mother.

The day before had been enjoyable for Mamie Bradley. After missing her child all week, she was pleased to get letters from Elizabeth and Emmett on Saturday. Elizabeth referred to Emmett as a nice, obedient, helpful boy. Emmett wrote that he was having a good time and that he would be home the next week. The letters lifted Bradley's spirits. Hosting friends that evening, she couldn't stop boasting about her Bo, saying she wished she could just go to Mississippi right then to bring him home.

At 9:30 Sunday morning, as she was getting ready for church, Bradley's phone rang. She answered. "Hello," she said. There was dead silence on the other end. "Hello," she repeated.

"This is Willie Mae. I don't know how to tell you. Bo."

"Bo, what?" She sat up. "Willie Mae, what about Bo?"

"Some men came and got him last night."

The news hit Bradley like a freight train. She asked Willie Mae questions—What had happened? What about the other boys?—but Willie Mae knew so little. Crying and distraught, Willie Mae soon hung up. Mamie became dizzy, her breathing heavy. She called her boyfriend, Gene, who rushed over to drive her to her mother's house. Though in no state to drive, Mamie took the wheel and blew through stop signs and red lights.

At her mother's house, Mamie tried to call Mose but couldn't get through, so they called the local newspapers. Soon reporters, as well as family and friends, filled the house. Then they called Uncle Crosby, Elizabeth's brother, who lived in a town near Money called Sumner. Mose's family had gathered there, and Crosby said he and Mose were about to visit the sheriff in nearby Greenwood. Crosby told Mamie that he would take care of everything and she should stay in Chicago. At Sunday services at Temple Church of God in Christ—a church that Emmett had found comforting, according to his mother—the congregation stood and prayed for his well-being.

Down in Greenwood that Sunday, Crosby and Sheriff Smith began to search under bridges and along riverbanks because, in Mississippi, that was were white perpetrators tended to dump their black victims. The search came up empty. Mose did tell Sheriff Smith that Roy Bryant was one of the kidnappers, so at 2 p.m. Smith drove to Money to talk to Bryant, who happened to be a friend of his. Bryant admitted that he and Milam had picked up Till, but he said they then let him go when his wife, Carolyn, claimed he wasn't the boy who had accosted her. Nevertheless, Smith arrested Bryant for kidnapping. Later in the day, J .W. Milam was arrested, joining Bryant in the Leflore County jail.

Bryant and Milam remained behind bars while Sheriff Smith and Talahatchie County Sheriff H. C. Strider built their case against the suspects. They also spearheaded the search for the body, but they were coming up empty.

Early on Monday, Wheeler was sent on a train back to Chicago. Bradley and others gathered at her mother's house. William Henry Huff, a prominent Chicago attorney for the NAACP, told Mamie he was on the case. Till's abduction became such a big story that numerous high-level officials, including Chicago Mayor Richard J. Daley and Illinois Governor William Stratton, became involved.

Chicago mayor Richard J. Daley joined the effort to find Till. *(Courtesy of AP Images)*

Despite their efforts, Emmett remained missing on Monday and Tuesday.

On Wednesday, on a quiet, late-summer morning, a white seventeen-year-old named Robert Hodges fished on the Tallahatchie River. Near the shore, he noticed a pair of knees sticking out of the shallow water. Afraid to go near the body, he instead notified the Tallahatchie County sheriff's office.

Deputies soon arrived on the scene. They pulled a badly mutilated corpse of an African American male—tied to a gin fan that weighed about a hundred pounds—out of the water. The sight was revolting: the naked body had swollen

Emmett's body was found in the Tallahatchie River, seen here. *(Courtesy of AP Images/Rogelio Solis)*

to nearly twice its original size, the neck had been ripped by the barbed wire attached to the fan, and one side of the forehead was crushed. One eye was gouged out, and the other dangled out of the socket. Many teeth were missing. Above the right ear was what appeared to be a bullet hole.

The corpse was beyond recognition, even for Mose Wright, who had been called upon to identify the body. Mose, however, did recognize the silver ring on the corpse's finger. It read, "May 25, 1943, L. T." Wright was certain it was the ring of Emmett's late father, Louis Till, which Emmett had always worn during his visit. That was good enough for Sheriff Strider. The search for Emmett Till was over, and murder charges were brought against Roy Bryant and J. W. Milam.

Although Emmett's corpse was mangled beyond recognition, Mose was able to recognize this ring on Till's finger. *(Courtesy of AP Images)*

In Chicago, Mamie's friend Ollie broke the news to her and her mother. Mamie began to take notes, writing down all the details, before putting her pen down to cry. Her mother sobbed and sobbed, and soon everyone in the house was crying. At that moment, Mamie realized that she couldn't rely on others to make it through this ordeal. "I could see that things were about to get very hard, more difficult than they had ever been," she wrote. "Impossible, really. And the only one I could count on would be myself."

four

North vs. South

Shortly after Mose Wright identified Emmett Till's mutilated body, Talahatchie County Sheriff H. C. Strider—an imposing 270-pound man—ordered that it be buried that day, Wednesday, August 31. The corpse was shipped to a nearby black funeral home, and workers began to dig the grave. Bradley, however, had different plans—she was not going to let her only son be buried alone somewhere in Mississippi.

Though she was in no shape to plan the specifics of the burial, Mamie Bradley had to shoulder the burden. She had no husband, no siblings, and now no children, and her mother was even more distraught than she was. Claiming that the Lord gave her focus and strength, Bradley began to take charge. She contacted A. A. Rayner, the local mortician, and told him to try to stop the burial, to get Emmett's body back to Chicago.

"We were able to get that body out of Mississippi," Bradley said. "And I guess if we stopped and screamed ten minutes, the body would have been buried while we were screaming. But that same little voice told me, 'You do not have time to cry now. You will cry later. The world will cry for Emmett Till. Get the body out of Mississippi.' And that's what I did."

The grave was mostly dug when Sheriff Strider got the news. He agreed to ship the corpse back to Chicago, but he insisted that the casket remained sealed. Unbeknownst to Bradley, several people had signed official papers agreeing to keep the casket closed. Officials in Mississippi did not want the world to see how badly their citizens mutilated a northern black teenager. The seal of the State of Mississippi was adhered to the crate encasing the casket, and breaking it would not be allowed,—although Bradley would insist that it be broken and the casket opened. On Thursday night, Mamie's Uncle Crosby accompanied Till's body on a train ride back to Chicago. They rode on the *City of New Orleans,* the same train that Emmett had taken two weeks earlier.

Early Friday morning, Bradley arrived at the Twelfth Street train station. So, too, did friends, family, two bishops, the press, and hundreds of others. Chicagoans were outraged by the murder: one of their own had been killed by Southerners, and the victim was a likeable boy. The hate crime touched a nerve with Chicago's large black population, and the local media gave great play to the killing. Till's murder was such an important local story that Chicago's CBS affiliate had interrupted *I Love Lucy* to announce that Emmett's body had been discovered.

Bradley, pushed in a wheelchair because she was so distraught, watched as the crate was removed from the train

Overcome with grief, Mamie cries and screams upon seeing Emmett's coffin. *(Library of Congress)*

and placed on the bed of a truck. As she stood to touch the box, she fell to the ground, nearly fainting. Emmett's mother cried and screamed, her grief recorded by photographers and television cameras. As five men lifted the wrapped body out of the box, Bradley continued to wail: "Oh, God. Oh, God. My only boy. . . ."

The body, still wrapped, was placed in a hearse and sent to Rayner's funeral parlor. The stench of the five-day-old corpse was overpowering—so bad, in fact, that explosives were set off outside the funeral home to neutralize the smell. Rayner did not want Bradley to view the corpse, but she insisted. After morticians prepared the body for viewing, Mamie's father, John, and her boyfriend, Gene, escorted her into the room.

Composed, at least outwardly, Bradley examined her dead son. Feeling a need to start slowly, she began by viewing his feet, then his knees, then all the way up the body. Eventually she saw the face.

> I saw that his tongue was choked out. I noticed that the right eye was lying midway on his cheek. I noticed that his nose had been broken like somebody took a meat chopper and chopped his nose in several places. As I kept looking, I saw a hole, which I presumed was a bullet hole, and I could look through that hole and see daylight on the other side. And I wondered, Was it necessary to shoot him?

That night, rage simmered within Mamie Bradley, as well as within the black neighborhoods of Chicago. Folks had read about the kidnapping and murder. They had seen the grief-stricken mother on television. And on Friday evening, they flocked to Rayner's funeral parlor by the hundreds to express their grief and anger.

That night, until 2 a.m., the body was laid out for viewing, in an open casket, in the funeral parlor's chapel. Bradley had insisted upon an open casket so that the whole world could see what the murderers had done to her son. Endless lines of mourners, four abreast, passed the body of Emmett Till. Many wept; others fainted. Outside, a pamphlet was distributed entitled "Punish the Child Lynchers." Around midnight, Bradley addressed the crowd outside.

"This is not just for Emmett, because my boy can't be helped now, but to make it safe for the other boys," she said.

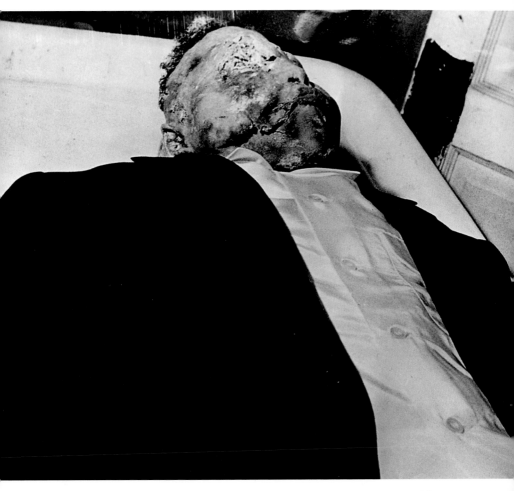

Mamie Bradley insisted on an open casket viewing so everyone could see Emmett's badly mutilated body. *(Courtesy of the* Chicago Defender*)*

"Unless an example is made of the lynchers of Emmett, it won't be safe for a Negro to walk the streets anywhere in America." She continued: "And it's the federal government's job to punish Mississippi for its refusal to protect colored people. I want to go to the Mississippi trial; I want other people to go with me to see this thing through. I'm willing to go anywhere, to speak anywhere, to get justice."

Lines of mourners continued to view the body throughout the weekend—an estimated 50,000 of them. *Jet* magazine, a national news magazine for African Americans, aroused passions by running a photo of Emmett Till's butchered face. All across the country, black Americans became sickened and incensed. So, too, were millions of white Americans.

In the early decades of the 20th century, prior to TV and radio, Northerners were largely ignorant of the injustices of the Jim Crow South. Then in the 1930s and 1940s, Northern whites were preoccupied with more pressing concerns—the Great Depression and then World War II. But in the prosperous 1950s, white Americans were more able to devote their attention to civil rights causes. The brutal murder of a black boy, just fourteen, from the North—publicized day and night on TV, radio, and all over the newspapers—inspired millions to demand justice. A *Chicago Sun-Times* editorial declared:

A large crowd gathers outside Roberts Temple Church of God in Christ during Emmett's funeral. *(Courtesy of AP Images)*

"A revolting crime against humanity has been committed in Mississippi. The senseless killing of Emmett Till is a shameful blot not only on Mississippi but on America."

On Tuesday, September 6, Emmett Till was buried in Burr Oak Cemetery in Alsip, Illinois. On the same day, it appeared that justice was indeed being served: A grand jury in Tallahatchie County indicted Roy Bryant and J. W. Milam for murder. The indictment, extremely rare for white-on-black violence in the South, meant the case would go to trial.

Initially, prominent Mississippians denounced the murder. Governor Hugh White said his state deplored such conduct. The *Jackson Daily News,* which generally reflected the white-supremacy attitude of the South, stated on September 2: "Every responsible citizen in the state of Mississippi agrees that the murder was a brutal, senseless crime and just incidentally, one which merits not one iota of sympathy for the killers."

John N. Popham, a *New York Times* reporter, stated that newspaper editorials "from one end of the state [of Mississippi] to the other" denounced the killing, and that black Mississippians "heard on every side a strong and vigorous condemnation by white people." Bryant and Milam could not even find an attorney willing to represent them.

On the weekend before the funeral, however, Mississippians began to be deluged by the hostile words of angry Northerners, some of whom blamed southern society—not just two individuals—for the crime. NAACP Executive Secretary Roy Wilkins was especially critical. Wilkins stated that "it would appear from this lynching that the State of Mississippi has decided to maintain white supremacy by murdering children."

Roy Wilkins (left) shakes hands with Martin Luther King Jr. and A. Phillip Randolph. *(Library of Congress)*

White Southerners were deeply offended by such accusations. For more than a century, they had resented Northerners imposing their ideas on their society, trying to eradicate the southern way of life. The 1954 *Brown v. Board of Education* decision had put the South further on the defensive. Southerners also despised the NAACP, which they considered an agitator organization run by power-thirsty blacks and influenced by Communists. And, of course, Mississippians resented the implication that they were all a bunch of murderers.

Tom Ethridge of the *Jackson Daily News* reacted to Wilkins' claim with a vicious response: "[The nation] was further shocked by the carefully staged Congo circus at a Chicago funeral home, where a youngster's last rites were used as an occasion to collect funds for promoting further racial strife and perhaps to fatten the wallets of agitators."

When Sheriff Strider announced that he had received threatening phone calls and letters from the North, Mississippians were fuming mad. Once again in American history, a line was drawn in the sand. The case of Emmett Till had become another battle between the Yankees and Confederates.

Sheriff Strider, the man who had declared on August 31 that the victim's body was indeed Emmett Till's, contradicted himself. More interested in defending the South's honor than seeking justice, he announced that he no longer believed the body was Till's—that it was too big—and that the boy could still be alive. Strider was fully aware that such a proclamation could sink the prosecution's case.

Meanwhile, attorneys suddenly came out of the woodwork to defend Bryant and Milam. In fact, all five lawyers in the town of Sumner took on the case *pro bono*: J. J. Breland, J. W. Kellum, C. Sidney Carlton, John Whiten, and Harvey Henderson. Throughout the area, storekeepers set up collection jars, with the money going to the defense fund.

With the trial scheduled to begin on September 19, the defense didn't have much time to build its case. Yet, while virtually everyone believed that Milam and Bryant were guilty, the defense attorneys felt they would win. The reason: because the trial would be held in Tallahatchie County, Mississippi.

Since only registered voters could serve as jurors—and no blacks in Tallahatchie County were registered to vote— only whites would sit on the jury. Moreover, Mississippi did not allow women to serve on juries, thus securing a jury of white men. Historically, southern white juries virtually always had acquitted white defendants of crimes against African Americans. Moreover, with the North-versus-South aspect of this trial, jurors undoubtedly would be hoping for a southern victory. Sheriff Strider's proclamation of doubt about the body certainly would seal the deal for the defense.

The prosecution, meanwhile, was intent on pursuing justice. Gerald Chatham, a well-respected district attorney, headed a strong team orchestrated by Governor White, who wanted his state to appear respectable in the eyes of the nation. Chatham was joined by Robert B. Smith, the Mississippi assistant attorney general. Two other attorneys and two Highway Patrol inspectors contributed to the investigation. Sheriff Strider,

The jury for the Emmett Till murder trial. *(Library of Congress)*

who claimed to have received 150 threatening letters, refused to assist the prosecutors.

On the morning of Monday, September 19, more than 1,000 people gathered around the Tallahatchie County Courthouse for the opening of the trial. Approximately sixty reporters and cameramen, white and black, southern and northern, were in attendance. All three major networks had airplanes to retrieve film of the trial, which would be broadcast on the nightly news.

Outside the court, tensions ran high. Local whites stuck together, eyeing northern reporters with suspicion, if not contempt. Black reporters and other African Americans kept with their groups, many fearing for their lives. An unexpected heat wave—ninety-five degrees and humid by Monday afternoon—added to the tense atmosphere. "The air is heavy, dusty, and hot," wrote the *Nation*'s Dan Wakefield, "and even the silence has a thickness about it—like a kind of taut skin—that is suddenly broken with a shock by the crack and fizz of a Coke being opened."

When the doors were opened, only a fraction of the crowd was admitted into the courthouse, in which ceiling fans circulated the hot air. About 250 whites were allowed to witness the trial from a second-floor perch. Sheriff Strider had not wanted to admit any African Americans, saying, "There ain't going to be any nigger reporters in my court-room." Nevertheless, he was overruled by the judge, and fifty African Americans were allowed to sit in the back of the segregated courthouse.

Judge Curtis L. Swango led the proceedings. Graying, soft-spoken, and authoritative, Swango was respected for his impartiality—at least compared to the many blatantly racist

Judge Curtis L. Swango was known for his fairness in the courtroom. *(Courtesy of AP Images)*

southern judges of his era. Informal, Swango allowed smoking in the courthouse and even permitted a card table to be set up in the back for eight black reporters—much to the annoyance of Strider. The sheriff, taking the threats against him seriously, made sure his deputies searched all African Americans for weapons.

Defendants Roy Bryant and J. W. Milam sat together at a table up front. Their wives, grim-faced, sat behind them, while their four young children (two each) alternated between their moms' and dads' laps (later they would run around the courtroom, even shooting deputies with water pistols).

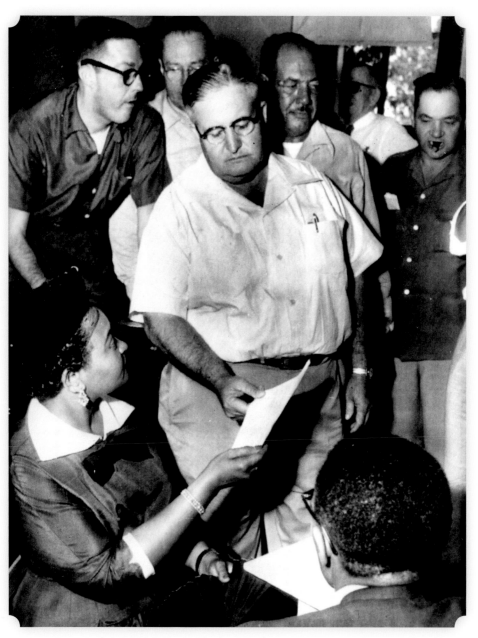
Sheriff H. C. Strider hands Mamie Bradley a subpoena to appear as a witness at her son's murder trial. *(Library of Congress)*

After allowing photos to be taken, Judge Swango ordered the attorneys to interview potential jurors. Prosecutor Chatham began with a surprising announcement. He said that because the state's evidence was largely circumstantial, and to ensure a fair and impartial jury, the state would not seek the death penalty. Chatham's news caused a ruckus in the courtroom, prompting the judge to bang his gavel.

In interviewing prospective jurors, Chatham asked them if they would be prejudiced because of the race of the defendants and of the victim. The defense attorneys, of course, also interviewed the potential jurors. Beforehand, however, they had talked to Sheriff Strider, who knew many of the potential jurors and helped the defense select those who would most likely acquit.

Some of the fifty jury prospects were disqualified because they admitted to contributing to the defense fund. By late afternoon, ten of twelve jury members had been selected—all male and all white. At this point, everyone in the hot, stuffy courtroom had had enough. At 4:30, Judge Swango announced that court was adjourned until the following morning. The trial was about to begin.

five
The Trial

Day two of the trial, Tuesday, September 20, irritated the local whites who packed the Tallahatchie County Courthouse. Nearly four hundred people shoehorned into a courtroom designed for far fewer, and the indoor temperature, according to one reporter, was a suffocating ninety-nine degrees.

The arrival of black congressman Charles Diggs (D-MI) added to the locals' aggravation. Sheriff H.C. Strider was less than welcoming. "I'll bring [Diggs] in here," Strider said, "but I'm going to sit him at you niggers' table."

The room fell silent when Mamie Bradley entered the court. Emmett's mother was flanked by her father, John Anderson Carthan, and cousin Rayfield Mooty, a labor leader in Chicago. Wearing a black dress and black veil, Bradley sat at the black press table, on which photographers climbed to take her picture. The *Jackson Daily News* scoffed at reports

A view of the segregated courtroom, with a card table set up for black reporters. *(Courtesy of Ed Clark/Time Life Pictures/Getty Images)*

that Bradley had risked her life going to Mississippi, stating she was less safe in "gang-infested Chicago."

Sheriff Strider continued his efforts to support the defense. For reporters, he produced a newspaper photo sent to him from an angry Chicagoan. In the photo, the defendants and Carolyn Bryant were covered with nail polish, slathered on to look like blood. "If the judge don't find them guilty," the letter read, "look for this to happen to all whites in Money, Miss."

Strider's efforts to acquit the defendants went well beyond his role of sheriff. Shortly after J. W. Milam and Roy Bryant were indicted for murder, Strider had locked up two possible witnesses to the killing, Henry Lee Loggins and Leroy "Too Tight" Collins, in the Charleston jail under false identities. They would remain there until after the trial.

Mose Wright identifies Milam and Bryant during his testimony. *(Courtesy of Bettmann/Corbis)*

The prosecuting attorneys were unaware of the gross breach of justice. Late Tuesday morning, in fact, after selecting the final two jurors, District Attorney Gerald Chatham asked Judge Curtis Swango to recess until Wednesday so his team, including NAACP workers, could locate and question more witnesses. The judge agreed, and a sticky, frustrated crowd headed for the exits.

After the sluggish Tuesday proceedings, day three began explosively. Chatham announced to the jury that the state had found six new witnesses who had seen Emmett Till with the defendants several hours after the kidnapping. Then the state called its first witness: Mose Wright.

Emmett's sixty-four-year-old great uncle pushed deter-
minedly through the crowded courtroom and took his seat on
the large, wooden witness chair. Wright, five feet three inches
tall, was nervous; he had received threats that he would be
killed if he took the stand. Yet Wright found the strength to
tell Chatham about the night of the kidnapping.

"Mr. Milam was standing at the door with a pistol in his
right hand and a flashlight in the other," Wright said.

Chatham interrupted: "Uncle Mose, do you see Mr. Milam
in the courtroom?"

Wright stood up. Then, in an action that was believed to
be unprecedented in the history of the South, the black witness pointed an accusatory finger at the white defendant in
question.

"There he is," Wright declared. Milam leaned forward,
cigarette in hand, and leered at Wright, but the old man was
not intimidated. He pointed then to the other defendant, adding, "And there's Mr. Bryant."

Before the crowd could react, Judge Swango pounded his
gavel and demanded order. Wright sat down hard. For the
remainder of his time on the stand, Mose Wright answered
questions in a strong voice and without hesitation, sometimes
pounding his fist on the table in front of him.

Wright recounted the details of the kidnapping, including a "light voice" at the truck affirming that Till was the
boy in question. He also said that he positively identified the
body as Emmett's because of the ring that remained on one
of the body's fingers.

After twenty-one minutes of testimony, Wright stepped
down from the stand. Soon, for his own safety, he would
leave his home state for good. Wright had defended his

great-nephew's honor, courageously, defying whites who had bullied him into remaining quiet earlier. He recalled that he could "feel the blood boil in hundreds of white people as they sat glaring in the courtroom. It was the first time in my life I had the courage to accuse a white man of a crime, let alone something as terrible as killing a boy. I wasn't exactly brave and I wasn't scared. I just wanted to see justice done."

After Wright's historic testimony, the state called several more witnesses. Included was Chester Miller, the black undertaker who had begun to prepare the body for burial before the decision to send it to Chicago. Miller described the damage to the body, although he said he could not confirm that the hole in the skull was from a bullet.

The murder trial in the death of Emmett Till attracted more people than the courtroom could hold. Among those present were three of the state's witnesses, (center row, left to right) Simeon Wright, Robert Wright, and Mose Wright, from whose home Emmett was taken on the night of August 28, 1955. *(Courtesy of Memphis Commercial Appeal/WpN)*

Robert Hodges, the teenager who had noticed the corpse in the Tallahatchie River, described the body as it was pulled out of the water. He said a heavy gin fan had been tied to the body with barbed wire around the neck. C. F. Nelson, a white undertaker, and C. A. Strickland of the Greenwood Police Department testified about the condition of the body. It was an anticlimactic ending to a historic day of testimony.

Emmett's body was found tied to this gin fan with a strand of barbed wire. *(Library of Congress)*

The next morning, while Americans read about Mose Wright's courage in their local newspapers, the most riveting day of testimony got underway. Chatham called Emmett Till's mother to the stand. Mamie Bradley walked from the back of the court to the witness stand amid a mix of sympathetic and hostile stares. For the honor of her son, Bradley knew she needed to keep herself together, keep her rage in check. She would talk properly, saying "yes, sir" and "no, sir." She would keep her cool at all times. And she would remain resolute in her belief that the dead body that she saw was definitely Emmett's—despite what Sheriff Strider had said.

Chatham soon asked Bradley about her viewing of the corpse at the A. A. Rayner funeral home. When she saw the body, she said, she knew it was Emmett's. "I looked at his face carefully," she said. "I looked at him all over thoroughly. I was able to see that it was my boy without a shadow of a doubt."

Chatham next handed Bradley the ring that was taken from a finger of the body. She not only confirmed that it was her son's but recalled when Emmett pulled it out of the jewelry box and put it on his finger before he left for Mississippi. When Chatham handed her a photo of the body, she began to cry while confirming it was her son.

During cross-examination, defense attorney J. J. Breland held up a photo of Till's body in the coffin and asked Bradley how she possibly could identify the mangled corpse as her son. She insisted she was absolutely sure. Breland then asked how much insurance she had on Emmett's life. She said about four hundred dollars. "Have you collected on the policies?" he asked. Despite the heartlessness of the veiled accusation,

Witnesses at the trial included (from left to right) Walter Reed, Willie Reed, Mamie Bradley, Congressman Charles Diggs, Dr. T. R. M. Howard, and Amanda Bradley. *(Library of Congress)*

Bradley responded courteously. "I've been waiting for the death certificate," she said quietly.

After Breland's next question—"Do you read the *Chicago Defender*?"—Judge Swango cut him off. The judge ordered the jury out of the room and then told Breland that every question he had asked would be excluded, for he was clearly trying to inflame the jury. Bradley stepped down from the witness stand.

In a hostile courtroom, with her son dead for just three weeks, Mamie Bradley had proved victorious—maintaining her composure, remaining steadfast that the body was her son's, and showing more class and integrity than the defense team. Yet, on her walk to the back of the courtroom, she noticed angry faces staring at her from every direction. She set her sights on the caring eyes of her father, who escorted her out of the room.

Willie Reed, the eighteen-year-old who had witnessed the beating of Till on August 28, took the stand next. Reed was clearly nervous and had to be told several times by Judge Swango to speak up. Nonetheless, Reed provided seemingly damning testimony. He told Chatham that he saw a truck of four white men and three black males drive onto Leslie Milam's property on Sunday morning.

Handed a portrait of Emmett Till, he said, "It looks like the picture of the boy I saw in the back of the truck." Reed testified that he saw the men carry Till into the barn, from where he heard screams and licks and hollering. He claimed he saw Milam leave the barn with a pistol. The defense tried to rattle the nervous witness, pressing him about the distance he had been from the barn. After his testimony, Reed, with the help of Congressman Charles Diggs, fled Sumner, and soon Mississippi.

After lunch, Willie Reed's aunt and grandfather supported his testimony: his aunt said she saw four white men going into Leslie Milam's barn, and his grandfather Add Reed testified that he saw Leslie Milam on the plantation that morning.

Just before two o'clock, Chatham announced that he had no further witnesses. After a recess, the defense moved that the jury be directed to return a not-guilty verdict, but Judge Swango overruled the motion. The defense then called its first witness: Carolyn Bryant.

The state objected to using Carolyn Bryant as a witness. Attorney Robert Smith said, "The Supreme Court has ruled many times that whatever happened prior to the time of a crime has no bearing on the case." The defense team's intention, of course, was to enrage the jury—to portray Mrs. Bryant as a victim and Emmett Till as a predator who deserved what he got. The judge ruled that Carolyn Bryant could testify but the jury would have to leave the room. As the twelve men left, those remaining in the courtroom eagerly awaited Mrs. Bryant's story.

The *Jackson Daily News* stated, "Mrs. Bryant testified with downcast eyes as she talked about something which seemed to offend her delicacy." With defense attorney Sidney Carlton questioning her, Carolyn Bryant explained what Emmett Till did after buying candy in the store:

"He caught my hand in a strong grip and said, 'How about a date, baby?'"

"What did you do then?"

"I turned around and started to the back of the store, but he caught me at the cash register."

"How did he catch you?"

"He put both hands on my waist from the side."

"What did he say?"

"He said, 'What's the matter, baby, can't you take it?'"

"Did he say anything else?"

"He told me, 'You needn't be afraid.'"

Bryant testified that Till had said "unprintable" words to her, adding that he had been "with white women before." She said that another African American came into the store and pulled Till out. She claimed that Emmett said goodbye and that he whistled at her—and that it was clearly a whistle, not the stutter that some had suggested.

Reporters took down every word of Carolyn Bryant's testimony, and it would dominate headlines and infuriate many the next day. The jury returned and, after brief informational testimony by J. W. Milam's wife, Juanita, the defense put Sheriff H. C. Strider on the stand.

Strider again did what he could to support the defense. He opined that the body had been in the river for "about ten days, if not fifteen," even though the body was found just three days after Till's kidnapping. Strider also said that, except for kinky hair, he couldn't tell if the body was black or white. He added that although he examined the wound over Till's right ear, he found no evidence of a hole in the skull—meaning a bullet hole.

The defense then put two more witnesses on the stand. Dr. L. B. Odkin of Greenwood said he believed the body had been in the water for eight to ten days. H. D. Malone, an embalmer, said, "The signs indicated to me he had been dead about ten days or longer."

The next morning, Friday, September 23, the defense rested its case. The final day was mainly comprised of closing arguments. Each of the five defense lawyers and both prosecuting attorneys spoke to the twelve-man jury.

A thunderstorm had rocked Sumner early Friday morning, but the courtroom remained hot and sticky. Prosecuting attorney Gerald Chatham, his sleeves rolled up, attacked the defense's claim that the body, and even the race of the victim, couldn't be identified.

"When the sheriff was first told of the body, his informer said, 'There is a little nigger boy in the river,'" Chatham boomed, his voice carrying through the windows. "But now we have this doctor come up here with all his degrees and title and tell us that he could not tell whether it was a white boy or a colored boy." Chatham added: "If there was one ear left, one hairline, one part of his nose, any part of Emmett Till's body, then I say to you that Mamie Bradley was God's given witness to identify him."

When Chatham finished his closing argument, Bradley said, "He could not have done any better." Defendants Milam and Bryant, however, were unmoved. While Chatham talked, Milam smirked and looked at a newspaper. Bryant lit a cigar. The jurors also appeared unfazed.

In his closing argument, defense attorney Sidney Carlton tried to cloud the issues of the trial. For one thing, Carlton said it was preposterous that Bryant would identify himself to Wright on the night of the kidnapping. "Had any of you gone to Mose Wright's house with evil intent, would you have given your name?" he asked. "There's nothing reasonable about the state's theory." He added, shouting his words: "If that's identification, if that places these men at that scene, then none of us are safe."

Defense attorney John Whitten tried to steer the jurors away from the facts of the trial, to base their decision on a

Bryant (left) and Milam (center) sit in court during their trial. *(Library of Congress)*

larger, if irrelevant, issue—the North trying to impose its will on the South.

"There are people in the United States who want to destroy the way of life of Southern people," Whitten said. "They would not be above putting a rotting, stinking body in the river in the hope it would be identified as Emmett Till." Defense attorney J. W. Kellum told jurors that "your forefathers will turn over in their graves" if they returned a guilty verdict.

After the conclusion of the closing arguments, Judge Swango retired the jury at 2:36 p.m., instructing them to return the verdict in writing. While the jurors deliberated, most of the large crowd remained in their seats. It was raining outside, and they expected a swift verdict.

At 3:43, bailiffs were informed that the jury was ready. As the jurors returned to their box, the judge asked if they had reached a verdict.

"We have," said foreman J .A. Shaw, Jr., a farmer.

"What is your verdict?" asked Swango.

"Not guilty," Shaw said firmly.

The spectators buzzed in conversation until Swango stared at them sternly. Defendants Milam and Bryant were immediately turned over to Leflore County officials for possible prosecution related to the kidnapping charge. For the moment, however, Milam and Bryant celebrated the verdict. They smiled, lit victory cigars, shook hands with well-wishers, and kissed their elated wives for the benefit of cameramen.

Outside the courtroom, hundreds of people milled about discussing the decision. A refreshment stand sold scores of sandwiches and soft drinks. Reporters dictated their stories over telephones while townsfolk listened in.

Milam and Bryant leave the courthouse as free men after being acquitted of murder charges. *(Courtesy of AP Images)*

Afterward, reporters garnered information from the jurors. Foreman Shaw said they had acquitted the defendants because the state had failed to positively identify the body as Emmett Till's. Another juror, in discussing the brevity of the deliberations—just sixty-seven minutes—said it would have been quicker had they not taken a soda pop break. Sheriff-elect Harry Dogan reportedly had informed the jurors to stretch deliberations to make sure no one suspected the jury of being prejudiced.

Few people that day were shocked at the verdict. In fact, Mamie Bradley didn't even show up because she was sure her son's killers would get off scot-free.

Sheriff Strider, who had hidden witnesses in a jail and lied about the identity of the body, got in the last word. Pointing a finger at a television camera after the trial, he said, "I just want to tell all of those people who've been sending me those threatening letters that if they ever come down here, the same thing's gonna happen to them that happened to Emmett Till."

six

Repercussions Around the World

As Roy Bryant and J. W. Milam were released on bail for their kidnapping charge, the murder trial's verdict became the talk of America. It had been the most celebrated kidnapping/murder case since that of the Lindbergh baby in the 1930s—and this time, the trial was on television.

The Till murder had shone a spotlight on the South's ugly customs of racism and segregation. The jury's acquittal was a display of obstinacy; Southerners showed that they would not let Northerners and African Americans infringe on their Jim Crow system. The day after the trial, many Southern white journalists tried to legitimize the trial and verdict. By doing so, they hoped to silence critics and close the book on what they deemed an unfortunate incident.

The *Delta Democrat-Times* stated, "Spectators at the Till trial, from wherever they came, must have been impressed with the decorum of our courts, the fairness of the judge and the sincerity of at least most of the officials involved." The *Greenwood Morning Star* wrote "that the top newsmen at the trial were unanimous in their opinions that the trial was fair and impartial." And the *Jackson Daily News* asserted: "Practically all the evidence against the defendants was circumstantial evidence. . . . Judge Curtis Swango presided with admirable fairness. . . . It is best for all concerned that the Bryant–Milam case be forgotten as quickly as possible."

But the story was not about to die so easily. Hodding Carter, the white editor of the *Delta Democrat-Times* (and a Pulitzer Prize winner) denounced the jurors' assertion that the identity of the body was in doubt. Carter wrote:

> The body was identified by relatives, was accepted by the boy's mother. . . . Had such a murder been planned to replace another body for Till's, the ring engraved 1943 L. T. (for the boy's father Louis Till), someone would have had to have been killed before the boy was abducted, the ring stolen from young Till and placed on the dead person's finger. Without the prior knowledge that Roy Bryant and his half-brother would kidnap Till, as they admittedly did, such a conspiracy defies even the most fantastic reality.

Virtually everyone, North and South, understood the truth: Milam and Bryant had murdered Till, largely because he was black, and the trial was a sham. Numerous journalists, politicians, and activists voiced their fury about the gross breach of justice, and irate citizens gathered en masse to protest the murder and verdict.

On Sunday, September 25, just two days after the trial ended, more than 60,000 people gathered at a rally in Detroit, where Congressman Charles Diggs and the NAACP's Medgar Evers spoke. In New York, 15,000 gathered to hear speeches

A rally in New York City was held to protest the verdict of the Emmett Till murder trial. *(Library of Congress)*

by Mamie Bradley and NAACP leader Roy Wilkins. *Jet* magazine editor Simeon Booker addressed 10,000 people in Chicago, while 3,000 came together in Baltimore.

The Till injustice inspired people to attend the rallies, but broader civil rights issues were discussed as well. Leaders called for enforcement of the *Brown v. Board of Education* ruling and the end of racial segregation. They demanded anti-lynching legislation and campaigned for black voting rights.

After the murder of her son, Bradley became a civil rights leader and spoke at numerous rallies. In this photo she attends a rally with her father, John Carthan. *(Library of Congress)*

Mamie Bradley suddenly became a civil rights leader, speaking in numerous cities. "I spoke from the heart about what it meant to send a boy away on vacation and bring him home in a box," she wrote. "And I spoke about Mississippi justice, where the laws seemed to be turned inside out.

Where innocent people were punished and guilty people went free."

At these rallies, people contributed to collections. Tens of thousands of dollars were raised to help the NAACP, the organization that had used much of its funds to fight the *Brown* case but needed more money for future campaigns. Also, in the wake of Till's death, membership in the NAACP rose dramatically.

At some of these rallies, leaders spoke not in generalities but about specific things that could be done to battle racial injustice. On October 11, U.S. Congressman Adam Clayton

U.S. congressman Adam Clayton Powell Jr. *(Library of Congress)*

Powell, Jr., a longtime black activist from Harlem, proposed a five-point plan to combat the recent murders in Mississippi (Till, Lamar Smith, and Reverend George Lee). Powell called for a special session of Congress to address the issue. He also suggested that the FBI send Northern FBI agents, including African Americans, to Mississippi to investigate the murders.

Powell's plan called for a national boycott of products from Mississippi He suggested that the NAACP, churches, and unions contribute to a modern Underground Railroad, which would escort black witnesses who testify against whites from Mississippi to the North. Finally, Powell proposed that no Mississippians be allowed in Congress, since the state refused to allow blacks to vote.

None of Powell's proposals would come to fruition. However, his concrete suggestions and those of other civil rights leaders were better than mere rhetoric. They made activists believe that real steps could be taken to overcome injustice.

Black newspapers closely covered the Emmett Till story, and inspired people to take action. The heavily read *Chicago Defender* declared on October 1:

> Whenever a crisis arises involving our lives or our rights we look to Washington hopefully for help. It seldom comes. . . . And usually, the Department of Justice seems more devoted to exploring its law books for reasons why it can't offer protection of a Negro's life or rights. . . . And Congress isn't concerned either. There has never been a congressional investigation of lynching, or of any other abuses and humiliations suffered by Negroes.

Readers of the *Defender* and other papers, numbering in the hundreds of thousands, realized that they couldn't rely on their government to fight injustice. They would have to do it themselves.

The Till case even sparked some southern whites to question Jim Crow customs. A September 26 editorial in the *Atlanta Constitution* insisted that if Milam and Bryant didn't

Eleanor Roosevelt

kill Till, Mississippi officials should find and prosecute those who did. "The burden remains with Mississippi and with the conscience of the people in the county or counties involved," the paper stated. "What will Mississippi and Sumner do about it so the Communists of Russia and of China may not say that in our country the law means one thing for one person and another thing for another?"

In fall 1955, it seemed that everyone had an opinion about the Till case—including Eleanor Roosevelt, widow of former President Franklin D. Roosevelt. Mrs. Roosevelt, one of the most influential women in America, wrote a piece in the

Memphis Press-Scimitar headlined "I Think The Till Jury Will Have Uneasy Conscience." She wrote: "I hope the effort will be made to get at the truth. I hope we are beginning to discard the old habit, as practiced in a part of our country, of making it very difficult to convict a white man of a crime against a colored man or woman."

The Till case, especially after the verdict, became international in scope. People from myriad nations criticized the United States, the so-called beacon of freedom and democracy, for oppressing its own people. This came during the Cold War era, in which many smaller nations remained unaligned, unsure whether to befriend the capitalist U.S. or the communist Soviet Union. The United States fought wars to prevent countries from going communist (the Korean War in the 1950s and the Vietnam War in the 1960s). Thus, ugly incidents such as the Till case could have profound geopolitical implications.

According to the American Jewish Committee (AJC),

> Europe's condemnation came from all sections of public opinion, all political directions, and was expressed immediately and spontaneously. Surprisingly, on this occasion the Communists were less vociferous than many of the liberal and conservative elements. These protestations were expressed in hundreds of newspaper editorials, statements by public leaders in every country of Western Europe, and by men in the street.

The Parisian weekly *Aux Ecoutes* was appalled by the trial, declaring:

> And this jury, which in spite of overwhelming proof acquits the two monsters, proving thereby that it consisted of men who are worth no more than the accused. And the judge who permits

that the two criminals hold on their knees two children who are being taught to hate the Negroes. And this country where no wave of indignation emerged after the acquittal.

Numerous other newspapers were critical of the Till case, including those in Italy, North Africa, and communist East Germany. Declared *Das FreisVolk* of Dusseldorf, East Germany:

Knowing that in the U.S. every hysterical woman can send a Negro to the electric chair by claiming that she was insulted, it is not surprising that until now no white man was ever sentenced to death in Mississippi because he killed a Negro. [Secretary of State John Foster] Dulles and the other roving preachers of American democracy and freedom who babble about the 'American way of life,' and who want to make us their satellites, have thrown a heavy veil over such freedom and democracy.

Finally, *L'Action,* the official publication of the leading nationalist party of Tunisia, North Africa, declared: "It is not enough for the U.S. to present itself verbally as the champion of liberty and justice. . . . This verdict is a shameless scandal which stains the justice of the U.S. It is one of those inequities that history does not forgive."

Back in the United States, many religious leaders, both black and white, spoke out against the trial. The publication *Christian Century* said:

Not often does anything happen in public life which is as unqualifiedly shameful as the double tragedy of the murder of Emmett Louis Till and the death of Mississippi justice in the ensuing trial. Bewildered, outraged, ashamed we all are; but most of all, Christians are sick: sick that such a crime should have happened in the first place; sick that such a judgement should have been handed down; sickest that in the back eddies of our nation slow, dark minds are taking satisfaction in the verdict.

Such criticism from a mainstream Christian publication was significant, as the United States was a predominantly Christian nation. Southern Christian leaders tended to condone segregation (indeed, churches themselves were segregated), while many ministers preached that whites, not blacks, were God's chosen people. Some white preachers spewed racial hatred.

As late as 1963, when white supremacists blew up a black church in Birmingham, Alabama, killing four girls, Reverend Connie Lynch said: "[The victims] weren't children. Children are little people, little human beings, and that means white people. . . . They're just little niggers, and if there's four less niggers tonight, then I say, 'Good for whoever planted the bomb.'"

In general, white religious leaders in the North disapproved of the South's Jim Crow system. Yet for decades, relatively few ministers or bishops or priests or Christian organizations spoke against the odious system. Now, with the Till story on the front pages, many of these leaders finally began to speak out.

Commonweal, a Roman Catholic journal, stated, "All over, people of every race and color read with shame and revulsion what had happened." *Commonweal* claimed that the racism that motivated the killers and permeated the trial "is the same disease that created the Northern ghetto in which he lived, [and] the Southern shack from which he was taken to his death."

Southern whites, on the defensive since the 1954 *Brown v. Board of Education* ruling, felt under siege. Everyone from the NAACP to the northern press to the Catholic Church to officials in North Africa were condemning their way of life. Southerners, feeling cornered if not persecuted, lashed back at their accusers.

One letter written to the *Memphis Commercial Appeal* attacked the NAACP:

> Because of the unfortunate incident at Sumner, Miss., the whole state of Mississippi has had her inalienable rights trespassed upon by critical eyes world-wide. She has truly become public fish bowl No. I. It was very obvious that the NAACP took every precaution to really place her in a tremendous 'hot spot' and they were very clever in their publicity endeavors.

Another letter to the editor stated that "the Negroes have no one but themselves to blame for what happened. Had Till observed the code and custom here, with which he was fully familiar, he would, without doubt, be picking cotton with his hosts in Sunflower County."

A third letter reflected the growing sense of isolationism that Mississippians were feeling: "It appears that every state outside Mississippi would have the world believe we live something like during the days of the Inquisition in Spain with dark dungeons, torture chambers, burning of possessed souls, etc."

Yet while Mississippians tried to deflect criticism, they continued to promulgate injustice. In November, Milam and Bryant were brought to trial in Leflore County on kidnapping charges. As in the murder trial, Mose Wright testified, recounting how Milam and Bryant had abducted Till. Willie Reed reiterated that he had seen Till in a truck with Milam the next morning. Leflore County Sheriff George Smith again testified that Bryant and Milam had admitted to taking Till from the Wrights' home in the middle of the night. Yet despite the seemingly damning evidence, a twenty-member grand jury acquitted the defendants. Jurors did not explain why.

Roy Bryant and J. W. Milam were free men. Because federal law states that an accused cannot be tried again for the same crime, Bryant and Milam were in the clear. If they wished, they could talk freely about the Till murder and even admit guilt without repercussion. In December 1955, they would do just that.

seven

The Killers Talk

I n the early 1950s, author William Bradford Huie wrote *Ruby McCollum: Woman in the Swannee Jail,* a best-selling exposé about a racially inspired murder. After the Emmett Till trial, Huie sensed another book opportunity—especially if he could get the suspected murderers to talk.

Huie, a seventh or eighth generation Alabaman, was conservative, yet also a champion of equal rights. In November 1955, Huie ventured to Sumner, Mississippi. He met with attorneys John Whitten and J. J. Breland, pleading for the chance to talk to their clients, Roy Bryant and J. W. Milam. Huie even offered to pay the suspected killers more than 3,500 dollars if they would tell their story. Paying for an interview/confession was highly unusual at the time, and by journalistic standards considered unethical. Huie later would defend the action by saying he simply was trying to find out the truth.

The attorneys pitched Huie's offer to Bryant and Milam, who accepted. The Fifth Amendment made them immune to double jeopardy, meaning they could not be prosecuted again no matter what they confessed, and Bryant and Milam were in desperate need of cash. Since the murder, African Americans had boycotted Bryant's store as well as businesses owned by Milam. Moreover, local white citizens were disgusted with the alleged killers, and they weren't anxious to help them

In 1955, author William Bradford Huie offered $3,500 to Milam and Bryant for their stories. *(Courtesy of AP Images)*

salvage their careers. Bryant and Milam also agreed to talk because they believed their actions were noble; they were not ashamed that they had killed whom they believed was an out-of-line northern black.

The attorneys were eager to arrange the meeting, Breland said, because they wanted to warn the nation— through the chilling words of the killers—that integration was unacceptable in the South. "The whites own all the property in Tallahatchie County," Breland told Huie. "We don't need the niggers no more. And there ain't gonna be no nigger integration. There ain't gonna be no nigger

The Fifth Amendment allowed Milam and Bryant to confess to murdering Emmett without facing legal prosecution. In this photo Milam (left) and Bryant (center) confer with one of their lawyers. *(Library of Congress)*

votin'. And the sooner everybody in this country realizes it, the better."

So, in the law office of Breland & Whitten, and then in a motel in Greenwood, Huie sat down with Bryant and Milam.

The older and more vocal Milam did most of the talking. Showing no remorse, Milam discussed the abduction and murder of Emmett Till. Milam's rendition of the kidnapping itself matched that of Mose Wright's. However, Milam was the first to explain what happened after they motored away from Mose's house at 2 a.m. on August 28.

Milam said he and Bryant drove across the Talahatchie River Bridge in Money and headed for Big River. There, they intended to pistol-whip Till and threaten to push him off a high bluff, which Milam called the "scariest place in the Delta." However, after a long search, they could not find the bluff in the dark. They then drove to J. W. Milam's house, arriving at 5 a.m.

No one was home, as Milam's wife and children were visiting her parents in Greenville. Milam and Bryant led Till into a tool house, where they began pistol-whipping him (a practice that Milam claimed he had inflicted on Germans while interrogating them during World War II). According to Milam, Till never hollered during his whipping. In fact, Millam said, Emmett told them: "You bastards, I'm not afraid of you. I'm as good as you are. I've 'had' white women. My grandmother was a white woman."

"Well, what else could we do?" Milam said. "He was hopeless. I'm no bully; I never hurt a nigger in my life. I like

Milam claimed he had pistol-whipped Germans while serving in the army during World War II. (*Courtesy of AP Images*)

niggers—in their place—I know how to work 'em. But I just decided it was time a few people got put on notice."

Milam told Huie that he would defend the southern way. He was not about to let his children go to school with black kids, nor would he stand by and let black citizens vote—otherwise, he said, they would take control of the government. "And when a nigger even gets close to mentioning sex with a white woman," Milam said, "he's tired o' living. I'm likely to kill him."

Milam said that after Till boasted about the white women he had been with, "I just made up my mind. 'Chicago boy,' I said. 'I'm tired of 'em sending your kind down here to stir up trouble. Goddamn you, I'm going to make an example of you—just so everybody can know how me and my folks stand.'"

Milam and Bryant easily could have killed Till right then, but a bigger concern was getting rid of the body. They decided they would tie a heavy object to Till after they killed him and then dump his body into a river. Milam and Bryant ordered Till back into the truck and drove several miles to the Progressive Ginning Company. There, Milam said, they made Till load a seventy-four pound cotton-gin fan onto the rear of the truck.

This admission was significant because it indicated that the murder was premeditated—not a killing that happened irrationally in the heat of the moment. Under normal conditions, those convicted of premeditated murder often receive the death penalty.

According to Milam, he and Bryant drove Till and the fan several miles to the Talahatchie River. Milam ordered Till to carry the heavy fan about thirty yards to a steep river bank.

"Take off your clothes," Huie quoted Milam as saying. Till followed the order.

"You still as good as I am?" Milam asked, pistol in hand.

"Yeah," Till replied.

"You still 'had' white women?" Milam asked.

"Yeah," Till said.

With that, he pointed his .45 at Till's head and pulled the trigger. The bullet entered near Emmett's right ear, and he dropped to the ground.

According to Huie, Milam and Bryant tied the gin fan with barbed wire to the body's neck, then rolled it into twenty feet of water. Milam then burned Till's clothes in his backyard—destroying, it seemed, the last bit of evidence.

Huie sold his story to *Look* magazine, and it appeared in an issue dated January 24, 1956. He found a hungry audience for his confessional piece, as it was excerpted in an April 1956 edition of *Reader's Digest*. It also was sold overseas and published as a chapter in a paperback titled *Wolf Whistle and Other Stories* in 1959.

Soon after publication, Huie's story—specifically, Milam's "confession"—was attacked as inaccurate. At every step of the abduction and murder, Milam had said that he and Bryant had acted alone. That, however, conflicts with the stories of several witnesses. Mose Wright had claimed that a person with a "light voice," presumably Carolyn Bryant, had accompanied Milam and Roy Bryant to Wright's home during the kidnapping. Also, Willie Reed had testified that he saw two white men and two black youths accompany Bryant, Milam, and Till to Milam's brother's plantation, where Emmett was beaten in a barn.

Moreover, James Hicks, a reporter for the *Amsterdam News,* a black newspaper, claimed that Henry Loggins and LeRoy "Too Tight" Collins were the black youths who were ordered to hold down Till in the back of the truck. After the trial, defense attorney J. J. Breland admitted that Loggins and Collins had been jailed under false names so that they wouldn't appear as witnesses.

Many readers particularly questioned Milam's portrayal of Till. Milam claimed that while he and Bryant were pistol-whipping him, Emmett didn't holler; and as they were about to execute him, he remained defiant. Doubters countered that even the bravest soldiers break down under such conditions—and Till was just a fourteen-year-old boy. Moreover, this was a boy who had burst into tears just hours before when he thought the car he was riding in had struck a dog.

Critics of Milam's story claimed he had tried to portray Till as uppity and remorseless, a black from the North who didn't respect white authority or the codes of the South. By depicting Till in this way, Milam believed he could justify the murder. After all, the killing of such disrespectful, out-of-line blacks had long been a socially acceptable punishment in the Deep South.

But while Milam thought he was describing Till as one worthy of execution, he actually portrayed him, in some people's minds at least, as a martyr. Proud African Americans, if they believed Milam's story, would recognize the courage of a young man who had refused to be intimidated or broken by whites—one who had remained defiant and courageous up until his death. In fact, by carrying the heavy gin fan to the point of his inevitable death, Till was seen as almost Christ-like—as if he were carrying a cross to his crucifixion.

The evidence suggests that Milam fabricated much of his confession, and not without reason. Had he said he had accomplices, they could have been arrested and charged with a felony. Even Carolyn Bryant could have been arrested for complicity in the kidnapping. By changing a few details of their crime, Milam and Roy Bryant still could give Huie the confession he wanted, walk off with the author's money, and not get anyone in trouble.

Despite the apparent inaccuracies, Milam's story proved valuable. It swiftly eliminated any doubts that he and Bryant were the killers. Thus, the excuses voiced by the supporters of the defendants—that no one could identify the body, that Milam and Bryant were upstanding men, and that the murder may have been a plot by the NAACP—now were proven false. With the killers' confession, Southerners no longer could attempt to justify what had happened. The warped system of justice—with racist sheriffs, attorneys, and jurors collaborating to oppress African Americans—had been fully exposed, stripped naked for the whole world to see.

Milam's confession also answered the question everyone at the time wanted to know: *How could the killers have done such a thing?*

Milam was a combat veteran of World War II, trained by the U.S. military to kill the enemy. The perpetrators' lack of sleep may also have been a factor. They had driven with and beaten Till throughout the night, from approximately 2 a.m. to 7 a.m., with no evidence that they took time to sleep. By morning, Milam and Bryant likely were frustrated and irritable, and certainly not levelheaded.

More significantly, though, like fellow white Southerners, Milam considered African Americans inferior to whites. As he said in his confession, "I like niggers—in their place." Clearly, Milam did not value the life of a black person. He also likely felt that he could have gotten away with the crime. Thousands of white men had killed blacks in the South over the years, and virtually all of them had walked away.

Milam said that he killed Till because the boy refused to submit. "You still as good as I am?" Milam said he asked Till moments before he shot him. "Yeah," Till said, according to Milam. "Well, what else could we do?" Milam told Huie. "He was hopeless." Thus, Milam murdered Till because he felt obliged to maintain the social order (white supremacy), and because he felt personally threatened by Till's challenge to his authority.

Milam and Bryant may have felt threatened by Till because Emmett's family was part of the Great Migration. With an abundance of factory work in the North in the 1940s and 1950s, hundreds of Southerners moved to such cities as New York, Chicago, Cleveland, and Detroit. There they found better wages and more personal freedom. The exodus of black laborers hurt southern landowners, who were compelled to raise wages for workers. From 1940 to 1948, the average hourly wage for picking a hundred pounds of cotton soared from $0.62 to $2.90. The black laborer no longer worked for whatever pittance his boss tossed his way; he now had bargaining power. With every wage increase, whites lost more money, more power over their black workers, and more of their grasp on the old way. It was enough to drive some Southerners, such as Bryant and Milam, to rage.

The threat of the *Brown v. Board of Education* decision in May 1954 also undoubtedly hung in Milam and Bryant's minds. With the integration of public schools, mandated

During the Great Migration, black laborers left the South for factory work in northern cities. *(Library of Congress)*

by *Brown,* Bryant's and Milam's kids would have to share classrooms—and school cafeterias, restrooms, and locker rooms—with black students. But Milam said "they ain't gonna go to school with my kids."

In fact, with growing national sentiment for equal rights, Southerners feared complete desegregation, including the end of all-white voting. That surely would lead to elected black officials and new laws that would strip whites of unjust power. But Milam insisted he would remain defiant. As he said, "Niggers ain't gonna vote where I live." According to

Milam, these were the reasons, noble reasons in his mind, that he made "an example" out of Till.

But Milam admitted there was another reason he murdered Emmett Till: "And when a nigger even gets close to mentioning sex with a white woman," Milam said, "he's tired o' living. I'm likely to kill him." Milam was no different than many other southern white men, taught for centuries that a black man defiling a white woman was an abomination, and the mere thought of it provoked vicious rage.

Interracial sex in the South had existed since the 1600s, but it was commonplace only among white men and black women—frequently white slave owners raping their slaves. According to the 1860 federal census, 588,532 Americans were classified as mulattos, meaning a racial mix of white and black, and the vast majority of them had white fathers and black mothers. White men rarely recognized or provided for their mulatto children, as white society was repulsed by the very thought of the two races interbreeding.

In the South, up to the 1950s, sex between black men and white women was extremely rare. It was, in fact, illegal. In 1892, Mississippi made interracial sex a felony, punishable by up to ten years in prison. In 1921, Mississippi legislators made it a crime, punishable to up to six months in jail, for even *suggesting* intermarriage. In some states, interracial marriage remained illegal until 1967, when the U.S. Supreme Court ruled that such laws were unconstitutional.

Traditionally, white women in the South were glorified. They were hailed as pure, virtuous maidens—southern belles to be protected against all that was vile. And the biggest threat of all, believed many white men, was the African American male.

For generations, whites stereotyped the black man as a "black buck," a "beast." The myth was that the black man could not control his sexual urges and that, if not kept in check, he would force himself upon women every chance he could.

Thus, with the white woman considered precious and vulnerable, and the black man deemed a sexual predator who would rape if given the chance, white men were often fanatical in their efforts to prevent interracial sex. In Yanceyville, North Carolina, black sharecropper Matt Ingram was convicted of assaulting a white woman from a distance of at least seventy-five feet. The assault was, in fact, an alleged leer. Just for looking at the woman, he spent two and a half years in jail.

A crowd gathers around the body of Rubin Stacy who was lynched for allegedly attacking a white woman. *(Courtesy of AP Images)*

Ingram was luckier than others. From 1882 to 1951, according to the Tuskegee Institute in Alabama, 534 African Americans were lynched in Mississippi (more than any other state). Many were lynched because they allegedly had raped, assaulted, kissed, touched, flirted with, talked to, or were within the vincinity of a white woman. Many of the

South Carolina governor Ben Tillman advocated lynching during his 1892 gubernatorial campaign. *(Library of Congress)*

allegations were just rumors, but that did not stop mobs from abducting and lynching the alleged perpetrators.

In 1923, a woman in Rosewood, Florida, said she was raped by a black man. Whites responded by killing blacks and burning down the whole town. Many other black men in the South were wrongly accused of assaulting white women, then arrested, prosecuted, jailed, and sometimes put to death.

During an 1892 gubernatorial campaign, South Carolina Governor Ben Tillman said, "Governor as I am, I would lead a mob to lynch the Negro who ravishes a white woman." In 1904, while governor of Arkansas, Jefferson "Jeff" Davis said: "I want to say that I would rather tear, screaming from her mother's arms, my little daughter and bury her alive than to see her arm and arm with the best nigger on earth."

Yet for all of the white man's fear of interracial sex, very few black men ever raped or had consensual sex with white women. For one thing, black men were too afraid of the consequences. York Garrett, who grew up in North Carolina in the early 1900s, said the black men in his community were afraid to even make eye contact with a woman for fear of being lynched.

In 1944, social scientist Gunnar Myrdal published *An American Dilemma,* which included interviews of blacks and whites. When asked to choose, from a list of six categories, what they thought blacks most wanted, whites listed "intermarriage and sex intercourse with whites" number one. Yet when African Americans were asked the same question, they put intermarriage/interracial sex *last* on the list.

Whites not only feared the "defilement" of white women but the results of interbreeding. Up until his death in 1947, U.S. Senator Theodore Bilbo (D-MS) warned against the "mongrelization" of the human race. Mixed-race children, according to Bilbo, were mongrels, a mixed and inferior breed. Many whites worried that a large number of mixed-race offspring would blur the color line and thus threaten the black-white caste system that defined the South.

All of these fears about interracial sex and mixed-race children remained in the South in the 1950s—if not as prevalently in progressive cities, such as Atlanta, then certainly in less-educated communities, such as rural Mississippi. By flirting with Carolyn Bryant and boasting of "having" white women, Emmett Till not only crossed a racial barrier but a racial/sexual barrier. In Money, Mississippi, in 1955, such a transgression provoked uncontrollable rage. And that, perhaps more than any other reason, was why J. W. Milam pulled the trigger.

eight
Rumblings

The verdict of the Emmett Till trial infuriated millions of Americans, prompting many to fight for civil rights. But what about the federal government? What were the Justice Department, Congress, the courts, and the President of the United States going to do to end racial injustice?

In the October 1, 1955, edition of the *Chicago Defender,* prominent black writer Langston Hughes wrote that the government owed African Americans its support:

> It would seem to me sort of nice if the white politicians in Washington would now repay those distinguished colored Americans who have sworn and double sworn their allegiance to democratic ideals, by investigating JUST A FEW of the white folks who hang fourteen year old boys to bridges and throw them in rivers, and who frighten and intimidate colored voters away from the polls—not to speak of those who continue to segregate the public schools.

After Emmett's murder, Langston Hughes urged the U.S. government to support African Americans. *(Library of Congress)*

In 1955, however, African Americans had few friends in high places. President Dwight Eisenhower seemed to care little about the problems of black folks. In the 1940s, he had opposed the desegregation of the military as well as the formation of the Fair Employment Practices Commission.

The president loved to play golf with white Southerners at the Augusta Golf Club, which banned blacks from membership. Politically, Eisenhower knew that if he championed

President Dwight Eisenhower did little to combat segregation and racism during his presidency.

desegregation in the South, he likely would lose numerous southern states in the 1956 election. Moreover, the president was so aggravated by the *Brown v. Board of Education* decision that he called his appointment of Earl Warren—the liberal Supreme Court justice who had championed the *Brown* desegregation ruling—the biggest mistake he had ever made.

Virtually everyone in the president's administration was white, and most of them considered black issues nothing more than a nuisance. Frederick Morrow, an African American advisor for the Commerce Department, was appalled by the White House's attitude. Max Rabb, the assistant to the president for cabinet affairs, "gave me a tongue-lashing on the Negro's attitude on securing his civil rights," Morrow wrote in early 1956. "He felt that despite what the administration has done in this area, Negroes had not demonstrated any kind of gratitude and that most of the responsible officials in the White House had become completely disgusted with the whole matter."

When it came to civil rights, the Washington heavyweights all seemed to pass the buck. Officials in the Department of Justice refused to get involved in the Till case, stating that it was the states' responsibility to protect their citizens. Such inaction angered civil rights activists, but during a cabinet meeting on December 2, 1955, Vice President Richard Nixon came up with an idea on how to deflect responsibility. He said the administration should challenge the Congress to pass civil rights legislation. Nixon added that any proposed bill likely would be watered down or killed by southern congressmen.

Many urged the FBI to get involved in the Till case, but the bureau's director, J. Edgar Hoover, was not interested. Hoover was a man who called members of the notoriously racist White Citizens' Council "some of the leading citizens of the South" and who, in the 1960s, spearheaded a smear campaign against Martin Luther King Jr. Hoover also distrusted the NAACP.

With little support for civil rights in Washington, it appeared that racial justice would never be served in the South. A low point came on December 3, 1955, when a cotton-gin manager, Elmer Kimbell, murdered a black gas station employee,

J. Edgar Hoover, director of the FBI, distrusted the NAACP and refused to investigate the Emmett Till case. *(Library of Congress)*

Clinton Melton, in Glendora, Mississippi. Kimbell was upset because he thought Melton had pumped more gas into his car than he had requested. Incredibly enough, the killer was driving the vehicle of J. W. Milam, his best friend! The trial received little national publicity, probably because Melton was (unlike Till) an adult and not from out of state. The jury acquitted Kimbell.

By this point, justice in Mississippi seemed hopeless. Hodding Carter wrote that the Till and Melton cases cemented the public's opinion that whites in Mississippi could always get away with killing an African American. In the wake of the Till and Melton murders—as well as the killings of Mississippians Lamar Smith and George Smith earlier in 1955—blacks in the state had ample reason to be afraid, and refused to challenge white authority. In fact, a White Citizens' Council reported in 1957 that Mississippi had "not one single school suit, or bus suit; and all is peaceful and serene with regard to race relations."

Yet while the White House was unwilling to take action, and black Mississippians were justifiably afraid to act, the Till case roused the American populace from its indifference to racial injustice. For many, the Till murder case was like a slap in the face. It caught their full attention, and they were ready to act.

In 1955, Anne Moody, an African American teenage girl in Mississippi, worked as a maid at a white family's home. Her boss, Mrs. Burke, told Anne that Till "was killed because he got out of his place with a white woman." She asked Anne how old she was, and she responded fourteen. "See, that boy was just fourteen too," Mrs. Burke said. "It's a shame he had to die so soon."

"I went home shaking like a leaf on a tree," Moody wrote. "For the first time out of all her trying, Mrs. Burke had me feel like rotten garbage. . . . Before Emmett Till's murder, I had known the fear of hunger, hell, and the Devil. But now there was a new fear known to me—the fear of being killed just because I was black."

Moody's experience prompted her to devote her life to the civil rights movement. She became one of the leading organizers of the Congress of Racial Equality (CORE), and she participated in numerous civil rights demonstrations.

Lew Alcinder, who set the NBA career scoring record after changing his name to Kareem Abdul-Jabbar, was eight years old in the summer of 1955. "The murder shocked me," he wrote. "I began thinking of myself as a black person for the first time, not just a person. And I grew more distrustful and wary. I remember thinking: They killed him because of his color. In a way, I lost my childish innocence." In 1968, Alcinder would lead a group of black American athletes that threatened to boycott the Summer Olympics.

Other young African Americans who would become prominent civil rights leaders of the 1960s were greatly influenced by the Till murder. They included James Forman, Stokely Carmichael, Robert Moses, and Medgar and Myrlie Evers. Some of the most influential black poets of the 1950s wrote

Medgar Evers (left) and Stokely Carmichael were greatly influenced by the Emmett Till murder and trial, and went on to become prominent civil rights leaders. *(Courtesy of AP Images)*

about the Emmett Till lynching. Langston Hughes penned *Mississippi—1955,* and Gwendolyn Brooks wrote *The Last Quatrain of the Ballad of Emmett Till.* In 1962, folk singer Bob Dylan released the song "The Death of Emmett Till." Though Dylan played loose with the facts, the song was significant because of Dylan's enormous influence on white America at the time—especially young activists on college campuses.

According to scholar C. Eric Lincoln, the Till case may have contributed to the swelling in membership of the Nation of Islam—a black organization that advocated a society separate from whites. Lincoln wrote that Nation of Islam members "very often use the Till case in their arguments against the white man's sense of justice."

Despite the White House's indifference to the Till case, some members of Congress were prompted to pass a civil rights bill—something that hadn't been done in Washington since 1875. Surely, the success of the Montgomery, Alabama, bus boycott in 1956 and the leadership of Martin Luther King Jr. inspired congressmen to pass civil rights legislation. But the Till case, and the effect it had on the American citizenry, also played a role. People would no longer stand by and witness injustices committed in the name of race, and urged their congressional representatives to change the laws that allowed people like Emmett Till's killers to go free.

Soon, a civil rights bill was on the floor of the House of Representatives, and then the Senate. Speaking to the Senate Subcommittee on Civil Rights, several witnesses discussed the Emmett Till case. On September 9, President Eisenhower signed the Civil Rights Act of 1957. The new act established a civil rights division within the Justice Department and called for the creation of the U.S. Commission on Civil Rights. It also allowed the federal government to bring suit against anyone interfering with another person's right to vote. Though civil rights advocates thought the act was too weak, with few provisions for enforcement, it at least was a step in the right direction.

For the first time in years, thanks in part to the Emmett Till case, Washington was doing something to help African Americans. Moreover, the impact of the Till case led to more than just a weak piece of legislation. It was the first rumbling, many historians have argued, of the civil rights movement.

nine
The Movement

Many historians list December 1, 1955, as the beginning of the modern civil rights movement. On her way home from work that day, a tired seamstress (and NAACP volunteer) named Rosa Parks refused to give up her seat to a white man on a segregated bus in Montgomery, Alabama.

Recalled Parks:

> When [the bus driver] saw me sitting, he asked if I was going to stand up, and I said, 'No, I'm not.' And he said, 'Well, if you don't stand up, I'm going to have to call the police and have you arrested.' I said, 'You may do that.'

Parks was arrested for violating a local bus segregation law. Four days later, the Montgomery Improvement Association was formed, led by Reverend Martin Luther

Rosa Parks *(Library of Congress)*

King Jr. That morning, in protest of Parks' arrest, black citizens in Montgomery staged a boycott of the city's bus system.

The Montgomery bus boycott lasted 381 days and led to the banning of segregated intrastate travel by the U.S. Supreme Court. The boycott proved to African Americans that, through mass protest, they could knock down the barriers to racial justice. Parks and King are hailed as the heroes of the boycott, but some historians believe that the Emmett Till case may have played a role in the Montgomery movement.

Black studies scholar Harvard Sitkoff asserted that for some black citizens in Montgomery, "who believed in the steady improvement in race relations, the moment of decision came with the August 1955 lynching of . . . Till and the brazen appearance of the White Citizens' Councils throughout the South." Added Mamie Bradley: "The black people of Montgomery were outraged and determined following Emmett's murder when Dr. King led the bus boycott there. They were moved by it."

The Till case may have even inspired Rosa Parks. "Someone asked Rosa Parks why she didn't get up when she was threatened," Reverend Jesse Jackson said. "She said she thought about Emmett Till, and couldn't go back anymore."

The Till murder and trial also seemed to have an effect on Martin Luther King. In a biography of King published in 1964, *Ebony* magazine editor Lerone Bennett wrote that the Till case "cauterized almost more radical departures. . . . The effect of all this on King, as on so many other Negroes, was explosive."

It is, of course, impossible to truly gauge the impact of the Till case on the civil rights movement. But certainly it fueled the flames, and from 1956 on the movement raged, sweeping across the South and changing the face of America.

In 1956, student Autherine Lucy attempted to integrate the University of Alabama, and black residents of Tallahassee, Florida, staged their own successful bus boycott. The next year, Martin Luther King led 30,000 people in the Prayer

Pilgrimage for Freedom, and President Eisenhower signed the Civil Rights Act of 1957.

In Little Rock, Arkansas, in September 1957, the National Guard escorted nine courageous students into Little Rock High School. They integrated the school despite hostile white mobs that tried to block the entrances. "Lynch her! Lynch her!" someone yelled at black student Elizabeth Eckford, but she and the rest of the Little Rock Nine refused to be denied their education.

Other black teenagers defied Jim Crow as well. On June 8, 1958, David Isom, age nineteen, jumped into a whites-only public swimming pool in St. Petersburg, Florida. The city, on the defensive, closed the pool. On September 16, 1958, two white teens in Little Rock tried to force Johnny Gray, fifteen, and his little sister off a sidewalk. Gray pointed a

This rally was staged to protest desegregation in Little Rock schools. *(Library of Congress)*

warning finger in one of their faces, then chased the two boys down the street.

On February 1, 1960, four black college students sat down at a whites-only lunch counter in a Woolworth store in Greensboro, North Carolina. They were refused service, but they sat at the counter until the store closed. The next day, more than seventy students staged another sit-in at the store. The story hit the newspapers, exciting young African Americans across the land, and by April sit-ins spread to dozens of cities throughout the South. Many were arrested, but they were willing to go to jail for justice.

On April 15, 1960, southern college students formed the Student Nonviolent Coordinating Committee (SNCC). The organization's members would organize more sit-ins and help get African Americans registered to vote. Most of SNCC's members had been about Emmett Till's age when he was killed, and his murder had affected many of them profoundly.

Cleveland Sellers, active with the SNCC in the 1960s, was eleven when Till was killed. He wrote:

> I read and reread the newspaper and magazine accounts. . . . There was something about the cold-blooded callousness of Emmett Till's lynching that touched everyone in the community. We all heard atrocity accounts before, but there was something special about this one. For weeks after it happened, people continued to discuss it. It was impossible to go into a barber shop or grocery without hearing someone deploring Emmett Till's lynching.

Julian Bond, who was approximately Till's age and was shaken by his murder, explained how he became interested in the movement:

Emmett Till's death had frightened me. But in the fall of 1957, a group of black teenagers encouraged me to put that fear aside. These young people—the nine young women and men who integrated Central High School in Little Rock, Arkansas—set a high standard of grace and courage under fire as they dared the mobs who surrounded their school. Here, I thought, is what I hope I can be, if ever the chance comes my way.

Bond became a founding member of SNCC and, decades later, the chairman of the board of the NAACP.

The sit-in movement, to which Bond contributed, was hugely successful at desegregating lunch counters and restaurants. On October 17, 1960, for example, Woolworth, Grant, Kress, and McCrory-McClellan announced they were integrating their lunch counters in 112 cities.

In December 1960, the U.S. Supreme Court ruled that segregation in interstate bus terminals was unconstitutional. So, in May 1961, the Congress of Racial Equality (CORE) tested the ruling by staging "Freedom Rides." Riding Greyhound buses through the South, racially mixed CORE groups attempted to use the whites-only restaurants and restrooms at terminals. White Southerners, however, were incensed. In Birmingham, Alabama, a white mob beat the riders bloody. In nearby Anniston, whites firebombed the riders' bus, smoking them out. In Montgomery, police stood by while whites attacked and clubbed Freedom Riders unconscious.

The Freedom Rides captured the nation's attention, winning empathy for the courageous riders and garnering hostility for racist Southerners. Newly elected President John F. Kennedy and his brother, Attorney General Robert Kennedy, pressured southern leaders to control their mobs. Meanwhile,

A group of Freedom Riders *(Library of Congress)*

the spirit among black freedom fighters surged. "I was hit over the head with a club," said black Freedom Rider Henry Thomas. "Even now my chest hurts and I almost conk out every time I climb a few steps. But I'm ready to volunteer for another ride. Sure. Any time."

Again, at least some of the Freedom Riders had been inspired to act by the Emmett Till murder. John Lewis, who was beaten unconscious in Montgomery, recalled years later, "I had witnessed through news accounts the lynching of Emmett Till." He described the details of the murder, then concluded, "That all had an impact on me." Lewis would become one of the "Big Six" leaders of the civil rights movement and, for two decades, a highly respected U.S. congressman.

In 1962, civil rights leaders staged a large-scale protest movement in segregated Albany, Georgia. At one point, activists there were unsure whether to defy a court order that prohibited marches on Albany's streets. However, at the Shiloh Baptist Church, Reverend Benjamin Welles told his assembly: "My name is being called on the road to freedom. I can hear the blood of Emmett Till as it calls from the ground. . . . When shall we go? Not tomorrow! Not at high noon! Now!"

In early 1963, Martin Luther King and Reverend Fred Shuttlesworth began a movement in Birmingham, Alabama, a city which King called the most segregated in America. Others called it "Bombingham" because of white supremacists' tendency to blow up the buildings of civil rights activists.

The memories of Emmett Till greatly affected Birmingham's black citizens. Reginald Lindsay, an African American who grew up in that city in the 1950s (and who would become a federal judge), recalled: "The mantra that was repeated to me (and I dare say to other boys my age) nearly every time I left my neighborhood, after August 1955,

In 1963, Birmingham's black citizens staged sit-ins and marches to protest segregation. *(Courtesy of AP Images)*

to go to a place where it was likely that I would encounter white people was: 'Be careful how you talk to white women. You don't want to end up like Emmett Till.'"

Birmingham's black citizens were sick of being oppressed and intimidated. In April and May 1963, they staged sit-ins and marches to protest segregation. On May 2, more than a thousand children, some as young as six, marched for justice. Public Safety Commissioner Bull Connor ordered his police to chase the youths with their attack dogs and his firefighters to blast them with water from their hoses, which was strong enough to knock bricks loose from their mortar.

"Look at 'em run," Connor boasted. "I want to see the dogs work. Look at those niggers run." Meanwhile, hundreds of the children were arrested, carted to jail in school buses. The atrocities in Birmingham shocked the nation, including the President. Kennedy told the press that he hoped that the violence in Birmingham "will remind every state, every community, and every citizen how urgent it is that all bars to equal opportunity and treatment be removed as promptly as possible." The hostilities in Birmingham ended in a truce on May 10, when civil rights leaders and local business leaders agreed on a desegregation plan.

More importantly, the Birmingham campaign spurred America's citizens, congress, and president to push for strong civil rights legislation. So, too, did the March on Washington, staged on August 28. Approximately 250,000 people, black and white, gathered peacefully in the nation's capital to demand justice.

Bayard Rustin, an activist who, along with A. Philip Randolph, was responsible for organizing the March on Washington, also had been inspired by the Emmett Till lynching. In his essay "Fear in the Delta," Rustin wrote about his visit with Amzie Moore, who in 1956 had taken Rustin on a tour of sites related to the Till murder: the barn where Till was beaten, the river in which his body was dumped, and the courthouse where the trial was held.

In summer 1964, SNCC's Robert Moses headed an ambitious project in Mississippi called Freedom Summer. Thousands of people, a mix of Mississippi blacks and white college students recruited from the North, helped get black Mississippians registered to vote. They also established Freedom Schools to give children an honest education.

Some whites responded to this violently, bombing Freedom Summer buildings and beating and killing activists. But unlike in the days of Emmett Till, many blacks refused to be scared into submission.

Fannie Lou Hamer had been a sharecropper in Mississippi most of her life. She was beaten by whites and involuntarily sterilized by a local

Fannie Lou Hamer *(Library of Congress)*

doctor. In summer 1964, she became one of the leaders of the Mississippi Freedom Democratic Party, which attempted to unseat the state's all-white delegation at the Democratic National Convention. In Emmett Till's lifetime, Hamer wouldn't have dared speak out against white racism. But in 1964, she broadcast her feelings to the world.

"We're tired of all this beatin', we're tired of takin' this," Hamer said. "It's been a hundred years and we're still being beaten and shot at, crosses are still being burned, because we want to vote. But I'm goin' to stay in Mississippi, and if they shoot me down, I'll be buried here."

The civil rights movement culminated in the 1964 Civil Rights Act and 1965 Voting Rights Act. Southern congressmen fought against the civil rights bill for months, but the bill had the support of most legislators, President Lyndon Johnson, and the majority of American citizens. Since 1955 Americans had heard horror stories of racial injustice from such activists as Mamie Bradley, Myrlie Evers, and Martin Luther King. They had witnessed such atrocities as the Till murder, the Freedom Ride beatings, and the attacks on children in Birmingham. Thus, on July 2, 1964, most Americans fully supported the signing of the Civil Rights Act by President Johnson.

The act banned discrimination in public places, and it barred unequal voter registration requirements, such as poll taxes and tests that southern whites had imposed on African Americans for years. The new law gave the U.S. attorney general more power to file lawsuits in order to protect citizens against discrimination. It required the elimination of discrimination in federally assisted programs. It established the Equal Employment Opportunity Commission (EEOC), and it authorized the commissioner of education to help communities desegregate schools.

The legislation was a great victory, but it fell short in ensuring blacks the right to vote. Though it banned poll taxes and understanding tests, whites in the South still ran the registrars' offices and voting precincts. They still had ways, such as intimidation, to keep blacks from voting.

In January 1965, Martin Luther King led a campaign in a small southern city to dramatize voting injustice. "This is Selma, Alabama," he proclaimed after being arrested there in February. "There are more Negroes in jail with me than there are on the voting rolls." Day after day during the Selma campaign, activists were arrested and beaten by police as they lined up outside City Hall to vote. During a peaceful demonstration gone awry in February, black activist Jimmie Lee Jackson was fatally shot in the back by a police officer.

In memory of Jackson and to protest voting injustice, activists staged a fifty-four-mile march from Selma to Montgomery on March 7. As six hundred marchers crossed the Edmund Pettus Bridge, mounted police routed them with clubs and tear gas. The event became known as "Bloody Sunday." Two days later, after a second aborted march, a white marcher, Reverend James Reeb, was killed by the Ku Klux Klan.

On March 21, King prepared to lead a third march across the Edmund Pettus Bridge. He told marchers: "Walk together children, don't you get weary, and it will lead us to the Promised Land. And Alabama will be a *new* Alabama, and America will be a new America!" Protected this time by federal troops, thousands of demonstrators marched triumphantly out of the city. For four days, thousands of black and white demonstrators—facing racist taunts but filled with pride—marched from Selma to Montgomery.

Inspired by the events in Selma, and urged by President Johnson, Congress passed the Voting Rights Bill. On August 6, 1965, Johnson signed the bill into law. The Voting Rights Act allowed federal workers to register black voters when necessary. And under the Johnson administration, the Justice Department was determined to enforce the new legislation. Three weeks after the Voting Rights Act was signed, federal officials registered more than 27,000 African Americans in Alabama, Louisiana, and Mississippi.

The following summer, Martin Luther King led a campaign in Chicago to end housing and job discrimination. By chance, he met up with Alma Carthan—Emmett Till's grandmother on his mother's side. "Mama happened to be driving by that place where he was staying, saw him, and stopped to talk," Mamie Till-Bradley said. "Just like that. She told me they talked about Emmett."

President Lyndon Johnson signs the Civil Rights Act of 1964. *(Library of Congress)*

By the late 1960s, Jim Crow no longer reigned in the Deep South. Abuse of African Americans, by either white citizens or police, decreased dramatically. Black voter registration skyrocketed, and more registered black voters meant more black jurors—which led to fairer trials.

To be sure, resistance to integration continued in Mississippi for years. In 1966, for example, hundreds of black protesters were beaten and arrested in the Mississippi cities of Oxford, Philadelphia, Canton, and Grenada. But great progress was achieved as well. In fall 1964, for example, school integration was carried out in Jackson, Biloxi, and Leake County, Mississippi. And in 1969, Charles Evers became the first mayor of a racially mixed Mississippi town since Reconstruction.

Incidentally, Charles Evers' brother, Medgar Evers, had worked with the prosecutors of Roy Byrant and J. W. Milam, trying to find witnesses for the Till case. Medgar, like Emmett, was murdered by a white Mississippian, Byron de la Beckwith, in 1963.

Historians will forever debate whether the Emmett Till case was *the* event that triggered the civil rights movement. It is certain, though, that the case had a profound impact. It also is interesting to note the dates of the civil rights movement's watershed moments: The Montgomery bus boycott began exactly one hundred days after Till's last evening alive. The Civil Rights Act was signed ten years to the month after Emmett was killed. And the March on Washington, in which Martin Luther King delivered his legendary "I Have a Dream" speech, occurred on August 28, 1962—the eighth anniversary of Emmett Till's death.

ten

Fifty Years Later

Following the triumphant passage of the Voting Rights Act of 1965, the civil rights movement lost its energy. Martin Luther King Jr., the champion of nonviolence, was assassinated in 1968. Militant African Americans, with cries of "Black Power," inspired rioting in such major cities as Detroit, Los Angeles, and Chicago. Such tension caused well-off, white city-dwellers to flee to the suburbs, replacing sanctioned segregation with economic and social segregation.

In the South, life for African Americans gradually improved. With each passing year, more schools and public facilities became integrated. Atlanta elected its first black mayor, Maynard Jackson, in 1973, and Birmingham put an African American, Richard Arrington, in the mayor's office in 1979. Despite reluctance, and occasional hate crimes committed by the Ku Klux Klan and others, whites eventually adjusted to the integrated New South.

Emmett Till's killers—Roy Bryant and J. W. Milam—were ostracized. Shortly after the murder in 1955, local blacks boycotted the three stores owned by the Bryant-Milam family. Since they had catered mostly to black clientele, the stores all went under. Later, Roy Bryant went to the bank to withdraw his savings, and was confronted by a group of local white citizens who told him to get out of town.

Bryant struggled the rest of his life. He worked odd jobs in Mississippi for two years before moving to Texas. There he labored as a boilermaker for fifteen years, damaging his eyes so badly that he eventually went blind. In 1972, he moved back to Mississippi to manage a grocery store that his brother owned. Carolyn Bryant divorced him in 1979, and in 1994 he died of cancer.

After the collapse of his businesses, Milam tried to scrape out a living as a farmer. He failed, however, after banks would not loan him money and black laborers refused to work for him. He, too, moved his family to Texas and then back to Mississippi, where he worked in construction. Milam divorced his wife and, in 1981, died of bone cancer.

Mose Wright and Willie Reed, the two men who testified against the killers, fled Mississippi and never looked back. Reed moved to Chicago, while Uncle Mose found work in Albany, New York.

Mamie Bradley, just thirty-three when Emmett was killed, had most of her life ahead of her. She went back to school, earned a teaching degree, and began a long career teaching special education in Chicago's schools. In 1957, she married Gene Mobley and changed her name to Mamie Till-Mobley. Mamie also did what she could to honor the memory of her murdered son. She lectured at various venues, wrote a book,

Mamie Till-Mobley speaks during a rally in this 2000 photo. *(Courtesy of AP Images/Hattiesburg American, Barry Beard)*

and tried for years to get the FBI and U.S. Justice Department to reopen the case. They always declined.

U.S. Congressman Bobby Rush (D-IL), couldn't accept that no one had ever been convicted for Emmett's murder. Rush, who was eight when Till was killed and later became a prominent civil rights activist, filed a bill in February 2004 asking Congress to formally request that U.S. Attorney General John Ashcroft reopen the Till case.

The Justice Department responded that it couldn't prosecute the case because it was too old—the statute of limitations had passed. Rush, however, disagreed, pointing out that 18 U.S.C. 3282, a federal law, stated that "an indictment for any offense punishable by death may be found at any time without limitation." Rush told the press: "The federal government has the resources, it has the authority, and should have the will to reopen this case. Emmett Till cannot and will not rest in peace. Mamie Till-Mobley cannot and will not rest in peace until there's justice. We cannot rest in peace."

U.S. congressman Bobby Rush

Rush was fortunate to have the support of Senator Charles Schumer (D-NY), a member of the Senate Judiciary Committee—which has oversight of the Justice Department. Schumer was intrigued with the research of young filmmaker Keith Beauchamp, who had scoured thousands of documents related to the Till case in preparation for a documentary on the subject.

Beauchamp, in a meeting with Schumer, said he believed that at least fourteen people may have been involved in the kidnapping and murder of Till, five of whom were still alive. Beauchamp and his stacks of evidence convinced Schumer to act. The senator pushed the Justice Department to reopen the case, saying it was never properly investigated forty-nine years earlier.

"It is a stain and will be a stain on both the Mississippi law enforcement officials and the United States Justice Department that it took a young filmmaker to bring to light what *they* should have brought to light," Schumer said.

On May 10, 2004, in an announcement that made headlines nationwide, the U.S. Justice Department and the Mississippi District Attorney's Office stated they would reopen the Till case. The Justice Department pledged it would investigate whether any prosecutions remained possible under state law.

"The Emmett Till case stands at the heart of the American civil rights movement," said R. Alexander Acosta, assistant attorney general for the Civil Rights Division. "This brutal murder and grotesque miscarriage of justice outraged a nation and helped galvanize support for the modern American civil rights movement. We owe it to Emmett Till, and we owe it to ourselves, to see whether, after all these years, some additional measure of justice remains possible."

The Till case wasn't the first famous civil rights case to be reopened decades later. In 1994, prosecutors in Mississippi convicted Byron de la Beckwith for the 1963 murder of Medgar Evers. And in 2002, Bobby Frank Cherry was sentenced to life imprisonment for his role in a deadly church bombing in Birmingham, Alabama, which also occurred in 1963.

Five months after the Till case was reopened, the CBS news show *60 Minutes* aired an extra-long story on the investigation. According to *60 Minutes* reporter Ed Bradley, the Justice Department was focusing largely on two people: Henry Lee Loggins, age eighty-one in 2004, and the former Carolyn Bryant, now known as Carolyn Donham since remarrying. According to reports from 1955, Loggins (likely against his will) had assisted Bryant and Milam in restraining Till during the kidnapping, then was jailed by Sheriff H. C. Strider during the trial so that he wouldn't testify. However, Loggins denied any involvement with the kidnapping. "I wouldn't sit here and tell you no lie," he told Bradley. "I don't know nothing about that case."

Carolyn Donham refused to talk to Bradley or any members of the press. Though the resurfacing of the former beauty contest winner made for sensational headlines, it was unlikely she would be convicted for any crime. After all, she had refused to disclose her encounter with Till to her husband, who found out about it from someone else. Carolyn Bryant may have been the person with the "light voice" (according to Mose Wright) who accompanied Roy Bryant and Milam to Wright's home to kidnap Till. However, no one at the Wright residence was certain it was her. Moreover, Carolyn could claim that her husband and Milam *forced* her to go with them to identify Till.

In 2005, a year that marked the fiftieth anniversary of the Till murder, the Justice Department announced the first major

Emmett's grave was reopened during a second investigation into his murder. (*Courtesy of AP Images/M. Spencer Green*)

event of the new case: Emmett's body would be exhumed and an autopsy would be performed. Some family members objected, saying that Till should rest in peace and that the body was obviously his. Others supported the exhumation, claiming that federal authorities were finally handling the case correctly.

The body was exhumed on June 1, 2005, and an autopsy was performed. The reasons for the examination were to confirm that the body was indeed Emmett's and to determine the cause of death. On June 11, examiners announced that they had found what they believed to be bullet fragments in the body. The official autopsy report was released on March 29, 2007, and concluded that Till died of the gunshot wound to his head. He also suffered broken wrists and skull and leg fractures. A month earlier, a grand jury found insufficient evidence to indict Carolyn Donham on manslaughter charges.

Mamie Till-Mobley never got to see Emmett's case reopened. On January 6, 2003, she died of heart failure. Her death made national headlines, and 2,000 people attended her funeral at Apostolic Church of God in Chicago. Elderly Rosa Parks could not attend, but a letter that she wrote—read at the funeral—moved the congregation:

> Thank you for your courage and bravery to share your only child with the world. The heinous crime which murdered your boy, your baby at fourteen years of age, shall never be forgotten. The news of the crime caused many people to participate in the cry for justice and equal rights, including myself. The respect I have held for you since 1955 will always live with me. You were blessed among women to carry the mantle with grace and dignity.

She was buried next to Emmett, at Burr Oak Cemetery in Alsip, Illinois. Before her death, she visited the cemetery—visited her son—often, sometimes musing about bigotry, intolerance, and racial injustice in her country. But mostly she thought about Emmett, her Bo, who gave her a kiss and a loving smile before hopping on a train to Mississippi. He had gone to spend time with his cousins, to swim and fish, and to feed the cows and chickens. He returned on the same train as a corpse, a martyr, the victim of a crime so heinous that it ignited America's most important social-justice movement of the 20th history.

Emmett Till was, his mother said with pride, "a little nobody who shook up the world."

Mamie Till-Mobley standing before a portrait of Emmett in her home. *(Courtesy of AP Images/Beth A. Keiser)*

Timeline

1941	July 25:	Emmett Louis Till, son of Louis and Mamie Till, is born in Chicago.
1955	Aug. 21:	Arrives in Money, Mississippi, where he stays at the home of his great uncle, Mose Wright.
	Aug. 24:	Congregates outside Bryant's Grocery & Meat Market with other black youths; flirts with Carolyn Bryant, a white woman alone in the store.
	Aug. 28:	Abducted from Wright's home by Roy Bryant and J. W. Milam; beaten, murdered, and dumped in the Tallahatchie River.
	Aug. 29:	Milam and Bryant arrested on kidnapping charges.
	Aug. 31:	Corpse retrieved.
	Sept. 2-4:	Thousands view mutilated body in an open casket.
	Sept. 6:	Grand jury indicts Milam and Bryant for kidnapping and murder.